Chocolate Chip Challah

and Other Twists
on the
Jewish Holiday Table

◆ ◆ ◆

AN INTERACTIVE

FAMILY COOKBOOK

AN INTERACTIVE
FAMILY COOKBOOK

◆ ◆ ◆

written and illustrated by

Lisa Rauchwerger

Chocolate Chip Challah

* * *

and Other Twists
on the
Jewish Holiday Table

URJ Press • New York

Library of Congress Cataloging-in-Publication

Rauchwerger, Lisa.
    Chocolate chip challah and other twists on the Jewish holiday table : an interactive
family cookbook / written and illustrated by Lisa Rauchwerger.
       p. cm.
    Summary: A cookbook using the calendar of Jewish holidays as a framework to provide
meaningful ways to celebrate them. Includes stories and an illustrated cooking dictionary.
   ISBN 978-0-8074-1077-6 (pbk. : alk. paper)
    1. Cookery, Jewish—Juvenile literature. 2. Fasts and Feasts—Judaism—Juvenile
literature. 3. Holiday cookery—Juvenile literature. [1.Cookery,Jewish. 2. Fasts and feasts—Judaism.
   3. Holidays.] I. Title.

TX724.R37 1999
641.5'676—dc21

Copyright © 1999 by Lisa Rauchwerger
Manufactured in the United States of America
10 9 8 7 6 5 4 3 2

In loving memory
of my beloved grandfather,
Ernest Rauchwerger,
who taught me the importance
of Jewish family traditions
and great baked goods!

In loving memory
of my beloved grandmother, Ida Levin,
whose generous spirit lives on
wherever good foods are cooking.

To my mother,
who gave me my Jewish soul
and taught me how to cook.

Acknowledgements

Thank you to my "secret weapon" and number one food critic Carie, whose friendship and love, wisdom and Judaic knowledge, not to mention organizational skills made finishing this project possible. Thank you Mom, Dad, and Misha, Grandpa L., and Grandma R. for supporting me from the beginning and giving me the message that I could do anything.

A warm thank you to Sharon Wechter and Seymour Rossel, who believed in me and the power of smiling veggies! To my new editor Hara Person, who took up the slack and guided me through this exciting process, and to Michelle Young in marketing, whose enthusiasm was second only to my mother's, thank you. Also with the UAHC Press, thank you to Ken Gesser, Stuart Benick, Debra Hirsch Corman and Vivian Fernandez. To all my friends who listened patiently every time I bored them with another idea, who were brave enough to try out new recipes, and who never ceased to get excited about my work, thank you for supporting me through the rough times and reminding me it was all possible. Thank you to Jenny Kattlove for helping me test recipes, Geri Garfinkel for all your helpful hints, and to Abra Greenspan, Ronny Kempenich, Gayle Notowitz, Karen Schneiderman, and Leora Troper and family for allowing me to use your recipes (or the ones you found) for this book. Thank you to Mom and Dad, Auntie Ada, Grandma Rauchwerger, and Katka Futterweit for passing on to me pieces of family history and tradition and for letting me pass them on to the world. To Bubbe Rubinchik, Grandpa Rauchwerger, and Grandma Levin, for your inspiration, love, and wonderful recipes that will live on through this book, may your names be remembered for a blessing.

Contents

An Important Note to Our Future Chefs

In this book you will find all kinds of wonderful things: the Jewish holidays, their Hebrew and English months, food facts and holiday trivia, not to mention really fun pictures! There is also room at the end of each chapter to write or draw your own stories and holiday cooking experiences. This book has at least one recipe for each major holiday in the Jewish calendar. Some are easier than others, but all are delicious. This book is meant to be used with a parent or accompanying adult. Learn how to cook and bake with a big person helping you, and when you're older you'll be expert enough to do it on your own! Have fun, and enjoy the yummies! Happy creating!

Here are some important things to remember whenever you work in the kitchen:

Always get permission from an adult to use the kitchen.

Read the recipe from beginning to end before you start. Make sure you have all the ingredients and utensils you need. Then give yourself enough time to finish the recipe.

Always wash your hands and put on an apron before you start.

Ask a grown-up to turn on the oven or light the stove for you.

Always use pot holders to put cookie sheets in the oven and (of course) take them out.

Never leave a plastic or rubber utensil inside a pot or on the stove when the burner is on; the plastic will melt, and melting plastic is very bad for you to breathe or touch.

When you are finished using something, always put it away so you won't have a big mess to clean up when you are all done.

Always clean up the kitchen after you finish cooking. Help do the dishes and put them away so there will be more room to enjoy the delicious food you just prepared!

HAVE FUN!

An Important Note to Our Adult Readers

This book is a culinary journey through the Jewish year. Each chapter introduces a holiday or festival, beginning with Shabbat. There are recipes for each major holiday in the Jewish calendar. Each recipe title page is set up like a page of Talmud, with the recipe in bold at the center, the Hebrew month at the top, and commentaries in the margins. There is also a section in the back of the book with blessings.

All recipes in this book are kosher, meaning they use all kosher ingredients and do not mix milk and meat. For your reference, each recipe is labeled at the top either "Dairy," "Pareve," or "Meat." Some recipes are easier than others, so there will be things that only an adult should do. However, this book is meant to be used by children together with a parent or accompanying adult—that's YOU! It is meant as an interactive family cookbook, an opportunity to teach and learn about the holidays while spending time with each other within the richness of the Jewish tradition. The process is as important as the product, so share your own family history, stories, and traditions. Enjoy the wonder of participating with your child in the learning process. Have fun, and remember that you are making memories for your children! Happy creating!

Some important things to remember when cooking with little people:

It is always easier to cook with children when you have tried out the recipes beforehand.

Always read the recipe from beginning to end with the child before you start. Make sure you have all the ingredients and utensils you need. Then give yourselves enough time to finish.

Make sure YOU handle the more dangerous tasks, like lighting the stove or removing hot items from the oven. Show the child how to do it and teach the safety precautions so that when they are old enough, they will be able to do it themselves.

Always have a step stool or chair handy!

When you are finished using something, encourage the child to put it away so you won't have a big mess to clean up when you are all done.

Don't forget to share your own family stories and traditions, and feel free to experiment with ingredients to make your own versions of the recipes.

HAVE FUN MAKING MEMORIES!

Illustrated Index of Utensils

These are some of the tools you will use to make the recipes in this book.

Baking (Cookie) Sheets

Basting/Pastry Brush

Candy Thermometer

Chopping Knife

Dough Blender

Electric Beaters

Frying Pan

Hand Graters

Juicer

Liquid Measuring Cup

Measuring Cups

Measuring Spoons

Meat Baster

Mixing Bowls

Muffin Pan

Paring Knife

Pastry Wheel

Potato Masher

Pot Holders

Pot with Lid

Rolling Pin

Rubber Scraper

Saucepan

Slotted Spoon

Spatula

Strainer

Vegetable Peeler

Wooden Spoon

NOTE: Look for these utensil icons at the top of each recipe. They will help you remember which ones to use!

Cooking and Baking Words to Know

Here are some words you will need to know when following these recipes.

Baste: to moisten (meat or other food) while cooking

Beat: to stir (eggs, etc.) vigorously, usually with a hand-powered or electric mixer

Blend: to mix smoothly together

Boil: to heat water or another liquid to the point where it starts to bubble

Chop: to cut into small pieces

Combine: to join or mix together

Cut in: (butter) to mix in and divide into small pieces, usually with a knife or pastry cutter

Dice: to cut into small cubes

Dissolve : to melt or liquify

Drain: to draw off a liquid gradually

Fold: to mix in or add by gently turning one part over another

Grate: to make into small pieces by rubbing against a sharp or rough surface, usually a grater

Grease: to cover with butter or oil, as in greasing a pan

Knead: to work (dough) into a uniform mixture by pressing and stretching

Melt: to change to a liquid state by heat

Mince: to cut into very small pieces

Parboil: to boil only partway

Preheat: to heat before using

Purée: to put through a sieve and/or blend smoothly

Rice: (to rice potatoes) to reduce to a form resembling rice; to grate very finely

Sauté: to fry lightly with a little oil or fat

Separate: (to separate eggs) to divide the whites from the yolks

Sift: to pass (flour, etc.) through a sieve to separate larger particles from small ones

Simmer: to cook at or just below the boiling point; almost boiling

Slice: to cut a thin, broad, flat piece; a piece cut from something

Stir: to move (usually a spoon) slowly inside a pot or bowl to blend or mix ingredients

Whip : to beat (eggs, etc.) to a froth; a dessert made with whipped cream or whipped egg whites

Wild challah in their natural habitat.

Shabbat

Shabbat is the Hebrew word for Sabbath, our day of rest. From Friday evening at sunset until Saturday evening at sunset is a time for Jews to be with loved ones and friends, enjoying the peace and quiet of nature and one another without the frenzy and frazzle that life and technology bring to our everyday lives. On Shabbat, we light candles, say blessings over challah and wine (or grape juice), and give thanks for a day of rest. We have special meals on Friday night and Saturday afternoon, and we don't do any work until sundown on Saturday. Baking challah on Friday mornings adds to the uniqueness of Shabbat. When I lived in southern California, I used to mix up my challah dough on Friday mornings, then place my bowl of dough in the passenger seat of my nice warm car and let it rise while I drove around town running my pre-Shabbat errands. After a while the dough would be fluffy and ready to be punched down! I would punch it down, then drive home, braid the challot, put the trays of braided challot back in my car, and finish my errands! It was my very own "challah-mobile"!

SHABBAT/Every Friday Night–Saturday

Pareve

Aunt Ada's Challah (With a Twist)

In 1939, when my father was only nine months old, his parents and aunt and uncle fled Nazi-occupied Czechoslovakia and sailed to South America, one of the few countries taking in Jews at that time. The two families shared a home and a farm, and my Great-Aunt Ada and my grandmother used to make this challah together every week. Later, when Aunt Ada moved to New York, she made this challah every Friday until she was in her mid-nineties! She handed down the recipe to me, and I filled in the blanks. (She knew the recipe so well she left out a few minor instructions, like "let it rise" and "punch it down.") This is a slightly sweet challah, wonderful for Shabbat and Yom Tov. And the secret ingredient is . . . a potato!

INGREDIENTS
1 small potato
4¹/2–5¹/2 c. flour
1 cup very warm water
(105°–115°)
1 t. sugar
2 pkgs. active dry yeast
(room temp.)
1 whole egg + 2 yolks
¹/2 c. oil (+ 1 t. for bowl)
¹/4 c. sugar
¹/4 c. honey
1 t. salt
oil/margarine & cornmeal
(for baking sheets)
1 egg yolk + 1 t. water
(for brushing)
poppy or sesame seeds
(if desired)

UTENSILS
ricer or fine grater
rubber scraper
wooden spoon
vegetable peeler
measuring cups/spoons
2 large mixing bowls
2 small bowls
baking sheets
1 small pot
pastry brush
liquid measuring cup
board or flat surface
candy thermometer
(optional)

MAKING THE DOUGH

❶ **Wash** and **peel** a small potato and **cut off** all "eyes" and bad spots. **Cut** into quarters and **boil** on medium heat until potato is soft, but not mushy. When poked with a fork, the fork should go in easily and the potato

TAKING CHALLAH
It is a *mitzvah* to pinch off a tiny piece of dough and bake it in the oven with the challah. This is called "taking challah." It symbolizes the loaf of bread given to the High Priests in the days of the Temple. Today it reminds us to give part of what we have to the hungry.

COVERING THE CHALLAH
Q. Why do we cover the challah on the Shabbat table?

A. *One explanation is so its feelings won't be hurt by being the last to be blessed. This teaches us that if we worry about the feelings of a challah, how much more so should we pay atten- tion to the feelings of other people.*

JOKE CORNER
Q. The Yiddish word *balabusta* (feminine) means "an excellent and praiseworthy homemaker". So what do you call a *balabusta* who makes challah every week?

A. *A Chalabusta!*

should just begin to fall apart. (You can do steps 2 and 3 while the potato is boiling.)

❷ **Measure** flour into large mixing bowl. **Start** with 4¹/2 cups of flour. (You will add more flour when you mix and knead the dough.)

❸ **Measure** 1 cup of water into glass liquid measuring cup and **put** cup in microwave **on HIGH** for about 1¹/2 minutes, or **measure** 1 cup of very warm tap water directly into measuring cup.

Water should be about 105°-115° f (warm but not boiling). **Spoon** 4 tablespoons of the warm water into a small bowl or cup. **Add** 1 teaspoon sugar to water. (The sugar in the water helps the yeast to rise faster.) **Empty** 2 packets of yeast into bowl and **gently stir** to **dissolve** yeast. **Set aside** for about 5–7 minutes to let yeast begin to foam. Yeast should **double in bulk.** Now **check** to see if potato is ready.

❹ When potato is ready, **drain** potato. **Cool** slightly, then grate pieces on very fine setting in hand-cranked grater or ricer into large mixing bowl with flour. (Potato pieces should be about the size of tiny rice grains, and grains should lose their shape when smashed with a fork.) **Mix** the potato and flour together.

❺ **Crack** 1 whole egg and 2 egg yolks into a small bowl. (**Crack** the 2 egg whites into a separate container and **save** in the refrigerator for breakfast or another recipe!) **Beat** the eggs slightly with a fork.

❻ **Add** yeast mixture to large bowl with flour and potato. **Add** beaten eggs and rest of warm water, ¹/2 cup oil, sugar, honey, and salt. **Mix together** all ingredients with a wooden spoon until well blended and dough no longer sticks to sides of bowl. You will need strong arms to do this! If dough is very sticky, add a little more flour until dough can be taken out of bowl without it sticking to the sides.

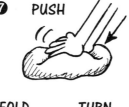

❼ **Turn out** dough onto clean, flat, floured surface. **Measure** a cup of flour and have ready to add to surface or dough. **Sprinkle** flour on your hands. Knead the dough, in a strong rhythm of **push-fold-push-turn, adding** flour to the board and/or your hands until dough is smooth, elastic, and no longer sticky, about 5–10 minutes. This is

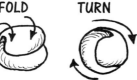

PUSH

FOLD   TURN

good exercise and a great way to let out your frustrations. I like to call it "challah therapy"! You can **test** the dough by **poking** your finger into the middle. If it bounces back, it's ready!

❽ Wash and **dry** the large flour bowl (and your hands) and **spread** 1 teaspoon of oil evenly onto the inside surface using a paper towel or piece of wax paper. (This will keep the dough from sticking to the sides when it rises.)

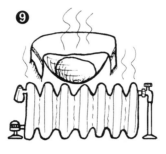

❾ Transfer dough to bowl. **Turn** dough so all sides are rubbed with oil. **Cover** bowl with a clean dish towel and **let** the dough **rise** in a warm place until doubled in bulk (about 1–2 hours).

WARM PLACES FOR DOUGH: In an electric oven (turned off) with the light on; on top of a radiator; under the covers of a water bed; in a warm car, etc.

BRAIDING THE CHALLAH
❶ Punch down dough. Use your fists to gently punch out all air pockets.

❷ FOR 4 SMALL CHALLOT: Empty out dough onto a floured board. **Pinch off** a tiny piece and **say**, "This is challah." When this tiny piece gets burned (by an adult!) in the oven, you will have fulfilled the mitzvah of taking challah! Now **divide** dough into 4. **Divide** each quarter into 3 equal parts. With your hands **roll out** each piece into a long cord. **Attach** them at the top by pinching the dough together. **Braid** them together, always crossing the outside strand over the middle one and alternating sides until you get to the end. **Pinch** the ends together. **Repeat steps** for each quarter. Now you have 4 small challot!

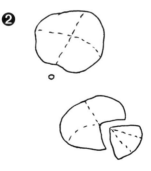

FOR 2 LARGE BRAIDED CHALLOT WITH CROWNS: **Empty out** dough onto a floured board. **Pinch off** a tiny piece. **Divide** dough in half. **Divide** each half into 4 equal parts. With your hands **roll out** 3 of the 4 pieces into long cords. **Attach** them at the top by pinching the dough together. **Braid** them together (for directions, see above). **Pinch** the ends together. Now **divide** the fourth piece into 3

parts, **roll** into cords, and make a smaller braid. **Place** the smaller braid **on top** of the larger braid, to make a challah crown! (**Fasten** the **smaller** one to the **larger** one with toothpicks, so it won't fall off while baking.) Now **repeat** these **steps** with the other half of the dough. Now you have 2 large crowned challot!

❸ **Grease** baking sheets with oil or margarine and **sprinkle** cornmeal on sheets. **Tip** the baking sheets and **lightly tap** them until the cornmeal sticks and lightly covers the

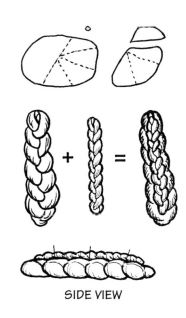

entire surface. **Place** challot and the tiny offering on baking sheets. **Cover** and **let rise** again in a warm place until doubled in bulk, approximately $1/2$ –1 hour.

Grandma Gisi (left) and Aunt Ada making Challah in Cumbaya, Equador, 1940.

❹ When challot are ready, **take out** a small bowl and **mix together** 1 egg yolk and 1 teaspoon water. (Remember to add the egg white to the other egg whites to use later.) With a pastry brush, **brush** challot with egg mixture and **sprinkle** with poppy and/or sesame seeds, if desired. (Brushing them with egg makes them look golden brown and shiny. The more water you use, the less shiny they will look.)

❺ **Bake** at 325° for about 30–45 minutes, or until golden brown. Carefully **test** them by lightly **tapping** the sides—if they make a hollow sound, they are probably done. **Remove** challot from baking sheets and **transfer** to wire racks to cool. (Extra challot can be stored in the freezer, wrapped in foil and placed in zip-top plastic bags. **Freeze** them the same day you make them. The day you want to use them, take them out and let them thaw naturally, or put them in the oven on very low heat. They will taste just as fresh as the day they were baked!)

CHALLAH IN SOUTH AMERICA

My Grandfather Ernest started his own bakery and pastry shop in South America, where he introduced the South American people to the dark bread and rich pastries of his native Czechoslovakia. There my grandparents learned how to braid challah using six strands instead of three, to make a complicated but incredibly beautiful braided challah.

SIDE VIEW

SHABBAT/Every Friday Night–Saturday

Meat or Pareve*

Chicken Soup with Matzah Fluffs

This is an easy and delicious way to have your soup and eat it too. If you choose the pareve bouillon, you can now enjoy a dairy dessert after chicken soup! And the matzah fluffs are so named because they come out light and fluffy and almost never round!

INGREDIENTS

SOUP:
10 c. water
1 large onion, chopped
2 stalks celery, chopped
2-3 carrots, peeled & sliced
    in rounds
1 T. fresh parsely, chopped
1 parsnip, peeled and sliced
    (optional)
1 clove garlic, minced
chicken-flavored bouillon
    (Telma or Osem) (vegetable
    bouillon* is OK, too)
1/2 T. margarine

MATZAH FLUFFS:
12 c. water
bouillon for 6-7 c.
2 T. margarine
2 eggs
1/2 c. matzah meal
1/2 t. salt

UTENSILS

SOUP:
1 large soup pot with lid
1 large saucepan
chopping knife
wooden spoon
measuring cups/spoons
vegetable peeler

MATZAH FLUFFS:
small bowl
electric beaters or fork
2 teaspoons

MAKING THE SOUP

❶ **Put** 10 cups of water **on to boil** in large saucepan. Meanwhile, **peel** and **chop** all ingredients. When water boils, **add** bouillon according to measurements on package (usually 1 teaspoon for each cup of water = 10 teaspoons).

❷ **Heat** margarine in large soup pot. When hot, **add** chopped onion and celery. **Stir** and **cover** for 3 minutes. **Uncover** and **add** carrots, parsley, parsnip (if desired), and garlic and **cover** for 3 more minutes. **Uncover**, and

---

DOCTOR'S ORDERS
Q. For years doctors have been prescribing chicken soup for their patients who have a cold or flu. What is another name for this Jewish miracle cure?

A. Jewish penicillin.

FLOATERS vs. SINKERS
A debate has been raging for centuries over whether a matzah ball is better if it floats or sinks. It is best to go with taste on this one. For the record, however, the matzah fluffs on this page are of the floating variety!

BLESSING THE CHILDREN
It is a *mitzvah* for a parent or parents to bless their child/ren at the Shabbat table.

NOTE THE QUOTE
"More than the Jewish people has kept the Sabbath, the Sabbath has kept the Jewish people."
—Ahad Ha-Am

"Floaters and Sinkers" or
"If matzah balls have a swim party in the fridge.
and no one is there to see it, did the party really happen?"

add boiling chicken stock. **Turn down** to simmer. **Add** matzah fluffs before serving.

MAKING THE FLUFFS:

❶ **Put** 12 cups of water **on to boil** in large saucepan. When boiling, **add** bouillon. **Cream** margarine in a small bowl with a fork or electric beaters. **Add** eggs and **beat** more. **Add** matzah meal and salt and **mix** evenly. DO NOT REFRIGERATE.

❷ **Spoon** fluffs directly into boiling stock using heaping teaspoons as measurement. **Keep** stock **boiling** until all matzah fluffs are in, then **cover** pot and **turn down** to a low boil. **Keep** pot **covered** for at least 1 hour WITHOUT LIFTING LID. Makes about 8–10 matzah fluffs.

SHABBAT/Every Friday Night–Saturday

Meat

Heavenly Honey Mustard Chicken

For all you mustard lovers out there, this recipe is quick and easy and oh so tasty! Serve with Shabbat Rice and steamed asparagus or broccoli for a healthy and delicious Shabbat meal.

INGREDIENTS
4 T. yellow mustard
2 T. spicy brown or Dijon
   mustard
2 1/2 T. honey
poppyseeds
3–4 chicken breasts
   (about 1 1/2 lb.)
non-stick cooking spray or
   vegetable oil
1/2 lemon
paprika

UTENSILS
measuring cups & spoons
small mixing bowl
tablespoon for mixing
baking dish
aluminum foil
pot holders

❶ **Preheat** oven to 350° **Mix together** mustards and honey in small bowl. **Stir** to blend. **Add** poppyseeds to taste.

❷ **Wash** and **place** chicken in a lightly greased baking dish. **Squeeze** fresh lemon juice on both sides.

❸ **Spoon** sauce over pieces. **Cover** both sides. **Save** a little bit of sauce for later. **Sprinkle** paprika on top.

❹ **Cover** with foil and **bake** at 350° for 30 minutes. **After** 30 minutes, **uncover**, **spoon** the rest of the sauce over the top, and **continue cooking** uncovered for 10 more minutes.

❺ **Remove** dish from oven with pot holders. Serves 3–4.

DID YOU KNOW. . .
Q. Which of the Ten Commandments speaks about Shabbat?

A. *The fourth commandment:* "Remember the Sabbath day to keep it holy. Six days you shall labor and do all your work, but the seventh day is the Sabbath of Adonai your God: you shall not do any work. . ."
         –Exodus 20:8–9

OUTLINE OF SHABBAT MEAL
This is the order of a traditional Friday night Shabbat dinner:

1) Light candles.
2) Sing "Shalom Aleichem."
3) Spouses bless each other.
4) Parents bless child/ren.
5) Kiddush over wine.
6) Wash hands.
7) Hamotzi over bread.
8) EAT!
9) Sing Shabbat songs—z'mirot.
10) Blessing after meal—Birkat Ha-Mazon.

SHABBAT/Every Friday Night–Saturday

Meat or Pareve*

Lisa's Shabbat Rice

This recipe has been enjoyed around the country and around the world, from California to New York to Jerusalem, even in the Midwest! It's simple and delicious. Enjoy!

INGREDIENTS
1 small onion, chopped fine
2 c. water
chicken flavored bouillon
   (Telma or Osem works well)
   or vegetable bouillon*
1 T. margarine
1 c. long-grain white rice

UTENSILS
1 medium saucepan with lid
small saucepan
measuring cups/spoons
spatula
chopping knife
liquid measuring cup

❶ Finely **chop** the onion.

❷ **Put** 2 cups of water to **boil** in small saucepan. When water boils, **add** bouillon according to measurements on package (usually 1 teaspoon for each cup of water = 2 teaspoons). **Stir** until bouillon is dissolved. **Keep** on medium heat.

❸ While stock is boiling, **heat** margarine in larger saucepan. When melted, **add** chopped onion and **sauté** until soft, not brown. **Add** rice and **stir** for 1 minute.

❹ **Add** boiling chicken stock to rice and onion, **stir,** and **cover**. **Turn down** to low and **keep** tightly **covered** for 20 minutes, until liquid is absorbed. DO NOT LIFT LID! After 20 minutes, **turn off** heat and **serve**, or **put** on warming tray with rice only partially covered, so it won't overcook. Serves about 4.

CANDLELIGHTING
Q. When do you light Shabbat candles?

A. Eighteen to forty minutes before sundown on Friday, depending on local custom.

DID YOU KNOW...
Many people traditionally light two candles on Shabbat, which correspond to the words zachor and shamor, "remember" and "observe." These words begin the two versions of the commandments for Shabbat: "Remember the Sabbath day and keep it holy" (Exodus 20:8) and "Observe the Sabbath day and keep it holy" (Deuteronomy 5:12).

Some people light as many candles on Shabbat as there are members in their immediate family.

END OF SHABBAT
Q. When does Shabbat end?

A. Shabbat is over when three stars appear in the sky.

My Favorite Things About Shabbat:

Set Your Own Shabbat Table:

Let the sweetness of the New Year carry you away!

Rosh haShanah

According to tradition, God created the world on the first of *Tishrei*, the first day of Rosh haShanah. The word *rosh* means "head," and *shanah* means "year"; hence this very important day is called "Head of the Year." The Yamim Nora'im, the ten "Days of Awe," begin with Rosh haShanah and end with Yom Kippur. During these very serious days, we think about the past year and decide what we can try to do better in the coming year. We apologize to everyone we may have hurt, and we take a close look at ourselves and our actions. On Rosh haShanah, we eat special foods, like apples and challah with honey, and we attend synagogue and pray for a good, sweet new year. The sound of the shofar, the ram's horn, wakes us from our spiritual sleep and reminds us to become better Jews and better human beings.

TISHREI/September–October

Pareve

Chocolate Chip (or Raisin) Challah

This is an extra special, sweet challah, wonderful for Rosh haShanah or to break the fast on Yom Kippur. And the secret ingredient is . . . a sweet potato! (If you have already mastered the Shabbat challah recipe, this will look familiar! I substituted a sweet potato for the regular spud, added a little more honey, and made 'em round!) But don't forget the raisins or chocolate chips! They make all the difference!

INGREDIENTS

2 pkgs. active dry yeast
    (room temp.)
1 t. sugar
1 c. very warm water (105°-115°)
1 whole egg + 2 yolks
1 t. salt
1/2 c. oil (+ 1 t. for bowl)
1/4 c. sugar
1/3 c. honey
4 1/2–5 1/2 c. flour
1 small sweet potato
chocolate chips/raisins
1 egg yolk + 1 t. water
    (for brushing)
margarine & cornmeal
    (for baking sheets)

UTENSILS

ricer or fine grater
rubber scraper
wooden spoon
vegetable peeler
measuring cups/spoons
2 large mixing bowls
2 small bowls
baking sheets
1 small pot
liquid measuring cup
board or flat surface
candy thermometer
    (optional)

MAKING THE DOUGH

❶ **Wash** and **peel** a small sweet potato and **cut off** all "eyes" and bad spots. **Cut** into quarters and **boil** on medium heat until potato is soft, but not mushy. When poked with a fork, the fork should go in easily and the potato should just begin to fall apart. (You can do steps 2 and 3 while the potato is boiling).

❷ **Measure** flour into large mixing bowl. **Start** with 4 1/2 cups of flour. (You will add more flour when you mix and knead the dough.)

❸ **Measure** 1 cup of water into glass liquid measuring cup and **put** cup in microwave **on HIGH** for about 1¹/2 minutes, or **measure** 1 cup of very warm tap water directly into measuring cup. Water should be about 105°-115° (warm but not boiling). **Spoon** 4 tablespoons of the warm water into a small bowl or cup. **Add** 1 teaspoon sugar to water. (The sugar in the water helps the yeast to rise faster.) **Empty** 2 packets of yeast into bowl and **gently stir** to **dissolve** yeast. **Set aside** for about 5–7 minutes to let yeast begin to foam. Yeast should **double in bulk.** Now **check** to see if potato is ready.

❹ When potato is ready, **drain** potato. **Cool** slightly, then **grate** pieces on very fine setting in hand-cranked grater or ricer, into large mixing bowl with flour. (Potato pieces should be about the size of tiny rice grains, and grains should lose their shape when smashed with a fork.) **Mix** the potato and flour together.

❺ **Crack** 1 whole egg and 2 egg yolks into a small bowl. (**Crack** the 2 egg whites into a separate container and **save** in the refrigerator for breakfast or another recipe!) **Beat** the eggs slightly with a fork.

❻ **Add** yeast mixture to large bowl with flour and potato. **Add** beaten eggs and rest of warm water, ¹/2 cup oil, sugar, honey, and salt. **Mix together** all ingredients with a wooden spoon until well blended and dough no longer sticks to sides of bowl. You will need strong arms to do this! If dough is very sticky, add a little more flour until dough can be taken out of bowl without it sticking to the sides.

❼ **Turn out** dough onto clean, flat, floured surface. **Measure** a cup of flour and have ready to add to surface or dough. **Sprinkle** flour on your hands. **Knead** the dough, in a strong rhythm of **push-fold-push-turn**, **adding** flour to the board and/or your hands until dough is smooth, elastic, and no longer sticky, about 5–10 minutes. This is good exercise and a great way to let out your frustrations. I like to call it "challah therapy"! You can **test** the dough by **poking** your finger into the middle. If it bounces back, it's ready!

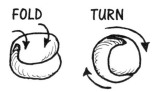

NOW FOR THE CHOCOLATE CHIPS OR RAISINS: Add chocolate chips or raisins to the kneaded dough, **pressing** them into the dough with your fingers and **distributing** them evenly. **Put more** than you think you'll need—when the dough rises it will expand and need more goodies!

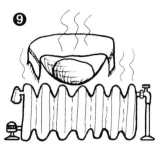

❽ **Wash** and **dry** the large flour bowl (and your hands) and **spread** 1 teaspoon of oil evenly onto the inside surface using a paper towel or piece of wax paper. (This will keep the dough from sticking to the sides when it rises.)

❾ **Transfer** dough to bowl. **Turn** dough so all sides are rubbed with oil. **Cover** bowl with a clean dish towel and **let** the dough **rise** in a warm place until doubled in bulk (about 1–2 hours).

WARM PLACES FOR DOUGH: In an electric oven (turned off) with the light on; on top of a radiator; under the covers of a water bed; in a warm car, etc.

BRAIDING THE CHALLAH:
❶ **Punch down** dough. Use your fists to gently **punch out** all air pockets.

❷ FOR 2 LARGE ROUND CHALLOT: **Empty out** dough onto a floured board. **Pinch off** a tiny piece. **Divide** dough in half.

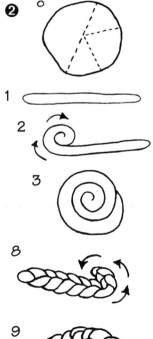

FOR SIMPLE ROUND COILS: **Roll out** each half into long cords. **Roll** cord **into** a **coil**, **starting** at one end and **rolling** coil around until you have a snail-shell-like round. **Tuck in** the **end. Repeat steps** to make 2 large, round, coiled challot.

FOR FANCY BRAIDED ROUNDS: **Divide** each half into 3 equal parts. **Roll out** into long cords. **Attach** them at the top and **braid together**, making a long braid. **Roll** braid **into a coil** and **tuck in the end. Repeat steps** to make 2 large, round, braided challot.

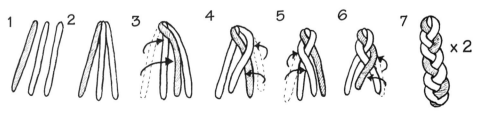

❸ **Grease** baking sheets with margarine and **sprinkle** cornmeal on sheets. **Tip** the baking sheets and **lightly tap** them until the cornmeal sticks and lightly covers the entire surface. **Place** challot and tiny offering on baking sheets. **Cover** and **let rise** again in a warm place until doubled in bulk, approximately $^1/2$ –1 hour.

❹ When challot are ready, **take out** a small bowl and **mix together** 1 egg yolk and 1 teaspoon water. (Remember to add the egg white to the other egg whites to use later.) With a pastry brush, **brush** challot with egg mixture. (Brushing them with egg makes them look golden brown and shiny. The more water you use, the less shiny they will look.)

❺ **Bake** at 325°–350° for about 30–45 minutes, or until golden brown. Carefully **test** them by lightly **tapping** the sides—if they make a hollow sound, they are probably done. **Remove** challot from baking sheets and **transfer** to wire racks for cooling. (Challot can be stored in the freezer, wrapped in foil, then double wrapped in zip-top or other plastic bags. **Freeze** them the same day you make them. On the morning of the day you want to use them, take them out and let them thaw naturally, or put them in the oven on very low heat. They will taste just as fresh as the day they were baked!)

TISHREI/September–October

Dairy* or pareve

Awesome Apple Cranberry Crisp

For a good, sweet year, try this classic comfort food. It's quick and easy and can be made dairy or pareve. Serve warm with vanilla ice cream!

INGREDIENTS
4 c. sliced tart apples
   (about 3–4 large
   Granny Smith)
about 1/3 c. orange juice
1/4 c. dried cranberries
2/3 c. packed brown sugar
1/2 c. flour
1/2 c. oats
3/4 t. cinnamon
2 dashes of nutmeg
1/3 c. butter or margarine,
   softened
butter,* margarine, or cooking
   spray (for pan)

UTENSILS
measuring cups & spoons
liquid measuring cup
assorted mixing bowls
chopping knife
vegetable peeler
knife/fork or dough blender
pot holders
8-inch square cake pan

❶ **Preheat** oven to 375°.

❷ **Grease** 8-inch square cake pan. **Peel** (optional) and **slice** apples, and **spread** apples evenly in the pan. **Pour** orange juice over the apples. **Sprinkle** the cranberries over the apples.

❸ **Combine** the topping ingredients in a small bowl, and **mix** with a knife, fork, or pastry cutter until the butter or margarine is in very small pieces and evenly coated. **Sprinkle** the topping over the apples.

❹ **Bake** at 375° for about 30 minutes or until golden brown, bubbly, and crispy. **Serve warm** with vanilla ice cream and hot apple cider.

TISHREI/September-October
Dairy

Rock-a-My Sole

Since it is customary for some Jews to eat fish on Rosh haShanah, I have included one of my favorites, bound to make even the fussiest fish eater into a believer! This one is oh-so-easy and tastes great! Enjoy!

INGREDIENTS
1½ c. cornflakes
¼ c. grated parmesan cheese
1½ t. parsley flakes
¼ t. onion powder
¼ t. garlic powder
Italian dressing, any kind
1 pkg. (about 1 lb.) fresh fillet
    of sole, or any similiar fish
    (roughey, turbot, cod)
1 fresh lemon

UTENSILS
food processor (optional)
shallow soup bowl
12" x 9" baking dish
tablespoon
measuring cups/spoons
plate
paper towels
pot holders

❶ Preheat oven to 325°.

❷ Crush cornflakes in a bowl with your hands, with a spoon, or in a food processor. Don't crush them too tiny! Pieces should be roughly the size of oats.

❸ Add parmesan cheese to bowl with cornflakes. **Add** spices, and **mix together** all dry ingredients.

❹ Pour Italian dressing onto a plate. **Set aside**.

❺ Rinse fish in cold water and **pat dry** between sheets of paper towel. **Place** fish in baking dish and **squeeze** lemon juice on both sides.

❻ Take out each piece of fish and **dip** it first in Italian dressing, making sure each side gets coated, then into the cornflake mixture. **Place** fish back in baking dish. You can **sprinkle** more crumb topping on parts that didn't get covered.

❼ Bake at 325° for 25 minutes or until edges start to get crispy and fish flakes when poked with a fork. **Remove** from oven and **serve** with rice or potatoes.

SOMETHING'S FISHY!
It is customary for some Jews to eat the head of a fish on the night of Rosh haShanah. Why? So that we may be like a head and not like a tail. What is special about a head? What kind of qualities does a head have that a tail does not?

POMEGRANATES FOR THE NEW YEAR
It is customary for some Jews to eat a pomegranate on Rosh haShanah. Pomegranates, mentioned in Song of Songs, have many tiny seeds, sometimes representing women's fertility. On Rosh haShanah, they symbolize the many mitzvot we hope to perform during the coming year. Pomegranates are also round, like the apples we eat with honey, representing the cycle of the year.

Our Family's Favorite Rosh haShanah Recipe/s:

Rosh haShanah Memories:

Left alone, fridge contents observe Yom Kippur.

Yom Kippur

Yom Kippur marks the conclusion of the ten "Days of Awe," or *Yamim Noraim*. It is a very serious day of fasting and prayer. We ask God's forgiveness for ourselves and for our community. Because we spend the day fasting, we enjoy a big meal before the fast begins, and we have a light, usually dairy "break the fast" after it is all over. Yom Kippur actually begins before sundown (but after the festive meal) and ends, like all Jewish holy days, after sundown on the following day. Can there be a Jewish holiday that does not involve eating? But it is because food is so central that we have a day set aside when we are specifically instructed not to focus on food. Instead, our attention is on matters of the soul, rather than the body. Yom Kippur is also called the "Day of Atonement." Atonement means saying you are sorry and being granted forgiveness. From Rosh haShanah to Yom Kippur, we ask our friends and family for forgiveness. On Yom Kippur, we ask God for forgiveness. But according to Jewish teaching, we can only be granted forgiveness by God for the things we have done against God. What we have done to hurt other people can only be forgiven if we have first confronted those whom we have wronged. After a long day of fasting and praying and thinking about what we have done wrong, it is time to eat again! So here are a few recipes for erev Yom Kippur (the evening before the fast) or to break the fast.

Tishrei/September –October

Meat

Diane's Roast Chicken and Potatoes

This is my mother's wonderfully tasty holiday standard, great for the festive meal before Yom Kippur. But go easy on the salt (especially with kosher chicken, which already has a lot of it) or you will be very thirsty when it comes time to fast! Mom doesn't use rosemary in her chicken, but I thought it might be a nice addition.

INGREDIENTS

CHICKEN:
1 whole chicken
2 whole lemons
onion powder
garlic powder
salt
pepper (fresh
    ground is best)
paprika
rosemary (optional)
hot water

POTATOES:
4–5 Russet
    potatoes,
or 14 new or
red skin potatoes

UTENSILS
roasting pan or
    baking dish
juicer (optional)
baster
large saucepan
paring knife

MAKING THE CHICKEN

❶ **Run** cold water over the chicken and **rinse well**, inside and out. **Dry well** with paper towels, inside and out. **Check** to make sure there is no paper left inside the chicken. **Place** chicken in roasting pan or baking dish.

❷ **Cut** lemons in half. **Squeeze** 1/2 lemon and **pour** juice on inside cavity of chicken. **Sprinkle** inside cavity with seasonings. **Squeeze** remaining 1 1/2 lemons. Starting with chicken breast side up, **pour** some lemon juice on chicken, then **rub** lemon half on breast and legs. **Sprinkle** with seasonings.

❸ **Turn** chicken over, breast side down. **Pour** remaining lemon juice over the back, wings, and sides of chicken and **rub** with lemon halves. **Place** squeezed lemon halves in chicken cavity. **Sprinkle** back, sides, and wings with sea-

TESHUVAH
Teshuvah means "returning." When we feel sorry about things we did and try not to do them again, we are doing *teshuvah*, returning things to the way they should be—turning ourselves back to God.

TEFILLAH
Tefilah means "prayer" and people pray in many different ways. Praying is talking to God, asking for help from a power greater than yourself, or thinking about ways to be a better person. Some like to pray alone; others prefer to join a group of people, or a *minyan*. Praying is sometimes like a long-distance phone call—we don't always get a good connection. But the more we do it, the easier it becomes. And the siddur (prayerbook) and machzor (High Holy Day siddur) help us know what to say.

sonings. **Keep** chicken breast side **down** in the pan. (This is the secret to keeping the breast moist.) **Add** a little hot water to the pan.

❹ **Set** oven to 325° and **roast** chicken for 1¹/2 hours, **basting** often. As pan juices dry, **add** more hot water. If chicken starts to get too dark, **cover** with a piece of foil.

MAKING THE POTATOES

❶ While chicken is roasting, **fill** a saucepan with water and **put** on the the stove **to boil. Wash** potatoes. If using Russet potatoes, **cut off** all eyes, **peel,** and **cut** into quarters. If using small red-skin or new potatoes, **do not peel. Cut** the larger ones in half but **keep** the smaller ones **whole. Parboil** potatoes in a large saucepan of water for 10–15 minutes, depending on size of potatoes (the larger they are, the longer you boil them). (Parboiling is boiling only partway; they will cook more in the oven.) DO NOT DUMP THE POTATO WATER!

❷ **Arrange** the half-boiled potatoes in the pan with the chicken. You can **use** the potato water **to add** to the pan juices as needed.

❸ **Baste** the potatoes as you baste the chicken. When everything is done, it will **keep** in a warm oven until ready to serve. Serves about 4.

TZEDAKAH

Tzedakah, from the root *tzedek,* means "right-eousness" or "justice," and a *tzadik* is a right-eous person, someone who feeds the hungry, helps the needy, and deals justly with every-one. When we give *tzedakah,* when we give to those less fortunate than ourselves, we must do it in a righteous and just way. That means respecting the honor of the person to whom we are giving it. It is so im-portant to know how to give justly that the philosopher Moses Maimonides came up with a system of levels of *tzedakah.* He called it the "Ladder of Tzedakah."

Q. Do you know what the highest (most righteous) form of tzedakah is?

A. *Helping persons help themselves.*
There is a saying that if you give a person a fish, you feed him/her for a day. But if you teach that person to fish, you feed him/her for a lifetime.

Q. What is the second highest rung on the Ladder of tzedakah?

A. *When the giver and receiver do not know each other's identity.*

Tishrei/September–October

Pareve

Abra's Magic Mandelbrot

Mandelbrot, "almond bread" or "almond rusks," is a crunchy, twice-baked Ashkenazi almond cookie, commonly served on Jewish holidays. It is a cousin of Italian biscotti. My teacher Abra Greenspan first shared this recipe with our Hebrew class about eighteen years ago. She was given the recipe by her mother, who got it from her mother, who in turn probably got it from her mother! This recipe is slightly different than others in that you only bake it once, so it's a little softer than traditional mandelbrot. Abra's mother used to make hers with chocolate chips. I like to make it with chocolate chips AND almonds.

INGREDIENTS	UTENSILS
3 eggs, beaten	assorted mixing bowls
3/4 c. oil	wooden spoon
1 c. sugar	baking sheet
3 c. flour	wire rack
2 t. baking powder	measuring cups & spoons
1/4 t. salt	liquid measuring cup
1 t. vanilla	
2–3 oz. chopped almonds and/or chocolate chips	
TOPPING:	
cinnamon & sugar	

❶ **Preheat** oven to 350°. **Beat** eggs in medium bowl. **Add** oil and sugar. **Stir together**.

❷ In a separate bowl **mix together** flour, baking powder, and salt. **Add** flour mixture to egg mixture a little at a time, **stirring** until blended.

❸ **Add** vanilla and chopped almonds and/or chocolate chips. **Mix** dough evenly. (This is hard work—use your muscles!)

❹ **Remove** from bowl and **form** dough into a log with your hands. **Transfer** to baking sheet and **flatten** with your hands into a long rectangular shape, about 1 inch high. **Even up** sides of dough.

❺ **Sprinkle** with cinnamon and sugar. **Bake** at 350° –375° for 10-15 minutes or until just lightly browned. **Cool** on wire rack. **Slice** and store in an airtight container.

HOLY DAYS
Q. What color robes do the rabbi and cantor wear on Yom Kippur?

A. *The rabbi and cantor wear white to recall the purity and sanctity of the day and to remember the white robes worn by the Kohen Gadol, the High Priest of the Temple in Jerusalem.*

KOL NIDRE
Kol Nidre, the service at the start of Yom Kippur, is the only evening service at which it is customary for congregants to wear a talit.

Evening services usually begin after the sun has gone down. But Kol Nidre begins right *before* the sun goes down.

Q. What does Kol Nidre mean?

A. "All vows."

BE HUMBLE
It is customary on Yom Kippur not to wear leather-soled shoes, because leather used to be a sign of wealth.

Vanishing Vienna Tarts

My Grandma Ida used to make dozens of these for every family gathering, and you would be amazed at how quickly they'd vanish! These lovely looking treats are perfect for break-the-fast, and can be made with low-fat cream cheese. Sit back and watch them vanish!

INGREDIENTS	UTENSILS
1 pkg. (8 oz.) cream cheese	large & small mixing bowls
2 sticks butter ($1/2$ lb.), softened	rolling pin
1 c. flour	measuring cup
jam, any flavor*	electric mixer
flour for work surface	pastry wheel
water	knife & teaspoon
	aluminum foil
*Not too runny is best.	spatula
	cookie sheets
	pot holders

❶ **Cover** bottom of oven with a sheet of foil. **Preheat** oven to 375°.

❷ **Cream** cream cheese and butter together in mixer. **Use** a knife to **scrape** the excess batter off the beaters when necessary. **Turn** beaters to low speed and **add** flour. Mix well.

❸ **Pour** some water into a small bowl and **set aside**. **Put** flour on your hands and **form** dough into a ball. **Roll out** dough with a well-floured rolling pin onto a well-floured surface. **Roll out** to $1/8$ inch thick. DON'T ROLL OUT TOO THICK. (The secret is to **use** enough flour on the board and rolling pin that the dough doesn't stick.) **Cut into** 2-

PASTRY WHEEL

VIDUI—CONFESSION

Probably the best known part of the Yom Kippur service is the *Vidui*, or "confession," where we rise and say we are truly sorry for all the things we have done, individually and as a community. We read aloud a long list of mistakes, or ways in which we have somehow "missed the mark" (to borrow a term from archery). We recite the *Al Chet* confessional (each line beginning with "For the sins WE committed before You . . .") in the plural, because when even a single person goes astray, the entire community is responsible.

CLOSING CALL

Q. What is the last sound we hear at the closing of Yom Kippur?

A. The sound of the shofar (ram's horn), blowing a *t'kiah g'dolah*, one very long, loud blast.

inch **squares** with a pastry wheel. **Collect** the excess dough into a ball and **set aside** to roll out again.

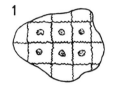

❹ **Spoon** a small amount of jam onto the center of each square. **Wet** two opposite corners of each square slightly with water and **fold** corners **over** the center, **sticking** the corners together to make an open-ended cookie. (Make sure the corners are well attached, or they will open up in the oven.) **Place** tarts on an ungreased cookie sheet. **Repeat** steps 3 and 4 until all the dough is used.

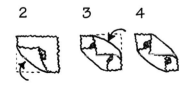

❺ **Bake** for 15 minutes or until golden brown. Makes about 25 tarts.

Our Favorite Food to "Break the Fast":

What Will I Do Differently This Year?:

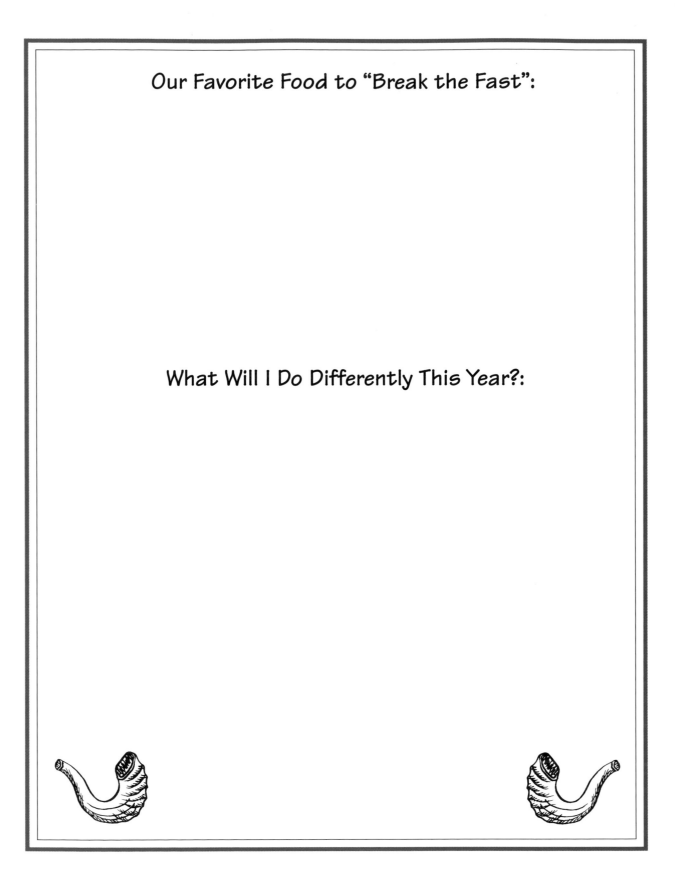

Edna Eggplant, Peretz Pumpkin, and Gary Gourd
prepare to decorate the sukah.

Sukot

When the days start getting chilly and the leaves begin to change colors, it is time for the harvest festival of Sukot. On Sukot, we build temporary shelters, *sukot,* and decorate them with seasonal fruits and grains. We eat our meals and sometimes even sleep in them. They remind us of the fragile huts built by our ancestors at harvest time and of the hasty dwellings our people used after the Exodus from Egypt. We remember that life, like the shaky *sukah,* is fragile, and we must give thanks for all that we have. During this week, we invite friends, family, and those who are hungry into our *sukah* to enjoy the holiday and to celebrate with us. Building and decorating your own *sukah* can be a lot of fun and a great way to spend quality time together with those you love. It's also a great excuse for a week-long picnic!

TISHREI/September–October

Dairy*

Puffy Pumpkin Pie

This special autumn treat is perfect for those starry nights in the sukah, or for hours after a Thanksgiving dinner when everyone is getting hungry again! It's light and fluffy and named for my beloved dog Puffy, who grew up with me.

INGREDIENTS (For One Pie)

PIE FILLING:

1¼ c. mashed cooked pumpkin
   (either 1 pie pumpkin or 1 can)
¾ c. brown sugar
1 envelope Kosher unflavored
   gelatin
½ t. salt
1 t. cinnamon
½ t. nutmeg
¼ t. ground ginger
3 slightly beaten egg yolks
¾ c. milk*, or soy milk
   (for pareve pie)
3 egg whites
⅓ c. granulated sugar
*whipped cream (even nondairy
   whipped topping is dairy!)

UTENSILS

assorted bowls
measuring cups & spoons
liquid measuring cup
food processor
wooden spoon
rubber scraper
9-inch pie pan
electric beaters
aluminum foil**
potato masher**
baking pan**

**If using fresh pumpkin.

GRAHAM CRACKER CRUST:

28 graham cracker squares (with 2 rectangles each)
¼ lb. (1 stick) butter* or pareve margarine
2 T. sugar
butter,* margarine, or nonstick cooking spray to grease pie pan

MAKING THE CRUST (Can be done ahead of time)

❶ **Grind** 28 crackers in a food processor until fine. **Pour** into large bowl.

❷ **Melt** butter or margarine in a microwave-safe dish in microwave or in a small saucepan on the stove. **Add** sugar to melted butter. Now **add** butter and sugar mixture to graham cracker crumbs. **Mix** until crumbs are evenly coated.

❸ **Preheat** oven to 375° (350° for glass pan). **Grease** 9-inch pie pan. **Pour** crumbs into pie pan and carefully **press down** crumbs with your fingers from the center, until bottom and sides are evenly covered.

❹ **Bake** 6–9 minutes until lightly browned. **Cool** at least 5 minutes.

MAKING THE PIE

❶ **IF USING FRESH PUMPKIN:** *(I highly recommend using fresh pumpkin over the canned variety—if you can spare the extra time. It is much tastier.)* **Cut** a pie pumpkin in half. **Remove** the seeds and stringy stuff. (**Save** seeds for roasting.) **Bake covered** with foil in a pan with a little water for about 1 hour at 350°–375°, until pumpkin is soft and thoroughly cooked. (Pumpkin meat should change color from light yellow-orange to dark orange.) **Scoop out** squash into saucepan and **mash** with a potato masher. If not soft enough, **cook** on low heat with a small amount of water until clumps separate and pumpkin is soft. **Measure** 1¼ cups. (Can be done ahead of time and kept in the refrigerator.)

❷ In a saucepan, **combine** brown sugar, gelatine, salt, and spices. **DO NOT HEAT YET.**

❸ **Combine** egg yolks and milk in a small bowl, then **stir** into brown sugar mixture. *NOW* **turn on heat** to medium and **cook, stirring constantly** until mixture comes to a boil. **Remove** from heat. **Stir in** pumpkin. (You may want to **transfer** mixture to a bowl.) **Chill** in refrigerator until mixture mounds slightly when spooned. **Test** now and then; if mixture gets too stiff, it is hard to fold in the egg whites.

❹ While mixture is cooling, you can **beat** the egg whites in a large bowl with beaters until soft peaks form. **Gradually add** granulated sugar, **beating** to stiff peaks.

❺ **Fold** pumpkin mixture thoroughly into egg white meringue. Carefully **turn into** graham cracker crust. **Chill** until firm. **Trim** with whipped cream right before serving. You can have fun decorating the top with different designs, but it melts quickly, so eat it soon after decorating! (Unfortunately, this is the only ingredient that cannot be made pareve; I found that even nondairy whipped topping is labeled dairy!

Roasted Pumpkin Seeds

These are a great snack when you need to munch! They're especially fun to make after carving all those pumpkins for Sukot!

INGREDIENTS
salt water for presoaking
1 c. pumpkin seeds
1 T. sweet butter* or olive oil
1/2 t. salt (optional)

UTENSILS
baking sheet
strainer
spatula
towel/paper towel
microwave-safe bowl/cup

❶ **Preheat** oven to 350°.

❷ **Presoak** seeds in salt water for about 1/2 hour or more. **Rinse** seeds well in strainer and **pat dry** on dish towel.

❸ **Melt** butter in microwave in microwave-safe bowl or cup, or in a small saucepan on the stove. **Stir** in salt.

❹ **Pour** salted butter mixture over seeds on baking sheet and **mix well**. **Spread** seeds out in one layer and **bake** on middle rack of preheated oven for 20–30 minutes or until they are golden brown and crisp.

❺ **Cool** on paper towel and **transfer** to tin or glass jar.

4 TYPES OF JEWS

There is a midrash that says that the arba'ah minim (four species of plants) used on Sukot represent four types of Jews. The etrog (citron) tastes and smells good, like a Jew who knows the Torah and does good deeds. The dates from the lulav (palm branch) taste yummy but have no smell, like Jews who know Torah but don't do good deeds. Hadas (myrtle) smells good but has no fruit, like people who do good deeds but don't know Torah. And the aravah (willow) has no taste or smell, like those who don't know Torah and don't do good deeds. (Maybe that's why the willow weeps!)

We hold all four close together to remind us that only when we all work together are we complete.

TISHREI/September–October
Dairy* or Pareve

Yentl (Lentil) Soup

For the hungry scholar in your life! This hearty soup is very satisfying on a chilly Fall or Winter's day. Serve with whole grain bread for a healthy, tasty meal.

INGREDIENTS
1/4 c. long grain white rice,
    rinsed and drained
6 1/4 c. hot water
Pareve chicken* or vegetable
    flavored bouillon
1 celery stalk, diced
1/2 onion, peeled and finely
    chopped
1 large or 2 small carrots,
    peeled and diced
1 t. fresh parsley, chopped
1/2 t. basil
1/4 t. celery seed
1 t. butter* or margarine
1 large garlic clove, minced
1 c. lentils

UTENSILS
1 large soup pot with lid
strainer (for rice)
spatula
wooden spoon
chopping knife
cutting board
vegetable peeler
liquid measuring cup
measuring cups & spoons

❶ **Measure** rice, pour into strainer, and **rinse** under water. **Set aside** strainer for rice to dry.

❷ **Put** 6 1/4 cups of water **on to boil**. When water is boiling, **add** bouillon for 6 cups and **stir to dissolve. Turn down** to simmer and **set aside**.

❸ **Chop** celery, onion, carrot, and parsley. **Measure** spices and **set aside**.

❹ **Heat** butter or margarine in pot. When hot, **add** celery and onion. **Stir, cover,** and **cook** 3 minutes over medium heat.

CHOL HAMOED
Many Jewish holidays that last for a week, like Sukot, begin with a day similiar to Shabbat, called a Yom Tov, or "holiday," during which we don't do the things we do on a regular day, like go to work, or school, or shop. The first day and the last day (and for some, the first and last two days) are considered Yom Tov, but the days in between are called Chol Hamoed, the "week-days of the holiday." During these days we continue to celebrate the holiday, but we do all the things we normally do during the week.

CHOL HAMOED SUKOT
During Chol Hamoed Sukot, we continue to eat and sleep in the sukah and shake the lulav and etrog.

❺ **Add** carrots, spices, and garlic; **stir**, **cover**, and **continue cooking** 3 more minutes.

❻ **Add** lentils and stock. **Bring to** a **boil**. Once boiling, **turn down** to low and **cook** soup **partially covered** a total of 2 hours over low heat, **stirring occasionally**. Liquid will evaporate and soup will slowly thicken and lose its color. About 20 minutes before it's done (after it has been cooking for 1 hour and 40 minutes), **add** rice and **continue cooking** 20 minutes more. **Remove from heat** and **serve**. Makes 4 servings.

Happy munching!

Our Personal Ushpizin List—
Whom Will We Invite/Whom We Invited
into Our Sukah:

What I Like about Being in a Sukah:

Go nuts, it's Simchat Torah!

Simchat Torah

Simchat Torah comes at the end of the long holiday season that starts with Rosh haShanah. On Simchat Torah, we read the very last *parashah*, or Torah portion, and the very first *parashah*. Reading them on the same day shows that there is no beginning and no end in the Torah. On Simchat Torah, everyone, even children, can have an *aliyah*, the special honor of reciting the blessings before and after the reading of the Torah. The word *aliyah* means "going up," and it is the same word used for moving to Israel. On Simchat Torah, we dance around the synagogue seven times with the Torah scrolls. Children make flags and put apples on the tops to show that Torah is sweet like an apple. Around this time, we also add a prayer for rain to our regular prayers. Simchat Torah marks the beginning of winter in Israel, and we pray for rain so that the farmers will have enough water for their crops. Now, in addition to flags, you can make your very own Torah cookies to enjoy on this happy day.

TISHREI/September–October

Dairy

Cinnamon Nut Torah Cookies

This was originally a rugelach recipe given to me by Gayle Notowitz. Rugelach is a rolled pastry that is a specialty of many Jewish bakeries. Here they are rolled individually to form little Torah scrolls. Roll only one side, and you have megillah cookies for Purim. They are fun to make and even more fun to eat! Go nuts!

INGREDIENTS
DOUGH:
2 eggs, separated into
    whites and yolks
1 t. + 1/2 c. sugar
1/4 c. very warm tap water
1 pkg. dry yeast
1 t. ground cinnamon
1 c. chopped walnuts
2 c. flour
1 c. butter or margarine,
    softened

GLAZE:
1/4 c. powdered sugar
1 T. milk

ETZ CHAYIM:
Cinnamon sticks,
sesame candies,
chocolate licorice, or
pretzel sticks

UTENSILS
assorted bowls
measuring cups/spoons
liquid measuring cup
baking sheets
spatula
pastry brush
mixing spoon
cooling racks
dough blender or knives
beaters
rolling pin
cutting board
table knife

MAKING THE DOUGH
❶ **Separate** the eggs into two bowls, **putting** the whites in one bowl and the yolks in another. Try not to get any yolk in the egg whites. (It prevents the whites from getting fluffy.) **Beat** the egg whites lightly.

Q. What is the Hebrew name for a scribe, a person who is specially trained to write a Sefer Torah?

A. A sofer sta"m.
סוֹפֵר סת"ם

Q. Sta"m in Hebrew is an acronym, a word formed from the initial letters of words in a phrase, like USA—United States of America. Do you know what sta"m stands for?

A. Sta"m stands for the three things a sofer is trained to write: **S**efer Torah, **t**efilin and **m**ezuzot.

DID YOU KNOW . . .
It takes a sofer working full-time for an entire year to write one Sefer Torah?

NOTE: As of this date, there are very few women scribes. However, there is no law that expressly forbids it, and there are several women who are beginning to challenge the tradition of only male sofrim.

❷ In another small bowl or liquid measuring cup, **dissolve** 1 teaspoon sugar in $1/4$ cup warm water. **Add** packet of dry yeast and **stir to dissolve. Set aside**.

❸ **Combine** $1/2$ cup sugar, cinnamon, and nuts in another bowl. **Set aside**.

❹ In a large mixing bowl, **add** flour and butter (or margarine). **Cut** butter **into** flour using 2 knives or a pastry cutter, until crumbs are all about the same size. **Add** egg yolks and yeast mixture (which has probably risen a little by now). **Beat** to form a smooth ball of dough.

❺ **Preheat** oven to 350°.

FORMING THE COOKIES

❶ **Roll out** dough on a lightly floured surface until dough is about $1/8$ inch thick. **Cut** into rectangles about $1 1/2$-2 inches wide and $6 1/2$-7 inches long.

❷ **Use** a pastry brush to **lightly brush** the rectangles with the slightly beaten egg whites. **Sprinkle** the nut mixture on top of each rectangle and **spread evenly**.

❸ Now carefully **roll up** the two ends, rolling toward the middle, leaving a small opening at the center. **Repeat** for each rectangle. Now you have little Torah scrolls! (If you make the rectangles shorter in length and roll up only one side, you have megillah cookies for Purim!)

  OR

ROLL UP BOTH SIDES FOR TORAH SCROLL   ONE SIDE FOR *MEGILLAH*

❹ Carefully **scoop up** cookies with a spatula and place on a well-greased baking sheet, about 2 inches apart. **Cover** with a clean cloth and **let rise** about 10 minutes. **Bake** at 350° for 15–20 minutes or until just lightly browned.

❺ While cookies are baking, you can prepare the glaze and the **atzei chayim**, the torah rollers.

TO MAKE THE GLAZE: Combine powdered sugar and milk, and **stir** until smooth. **Wash out** the pastry brush so it will be ready to use with the glaze.

TO MAKE THE ATZEI CHAYIM: Be creative with this part, and **use** whatever suits your taste buds! Items that have tested well include **cinnamon sticks**, cut short, **licorice whips** (chocolate-flavored ones go best), **sesame candies** (the little rectangular ones), or **pretzel sticks**. (I prefer the sesame candies!) For cinnamon, licorice, or pretzels, **break off** pieces about 3/4 inch long. For sesame sticks, **cut** each candy in half lengthwise and then in half again, widthwise, making 4 pieces. You will need 4 pieces for each cookie.

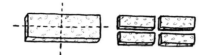

❻ When cookies are done, **remove** baking trays from oven and **turn off** heat. Gently **push** an *etz chayim* piece into each rolled end, just until it stays in place. **While** cookies are still **warm**, **brush** glaze on the rolled part of each cookie. **Transfer** cookies to a wire cooling rack.

Makes about 12–14 large cookies. Cookies can be frozen in a well-sealed container between sheets of wax paper.

TISHREI/September–October

Dairy* or Pareve

Pumpkin Date Muffins

When a child learns the alef bet for the first time, it is a tradition to put a drop of honey on the first Hebrew letter he or she learns, to show that the learning of Torah is sweet. This recipe is sweet and rich and can be made with children as young as three. The Torah can be sweet like dates, hearty and enduring with hidden secrets like a pumpkin, rich like butter, and full of exotic flavor and spice like cinnamon and nutmeg. Enjoy this modern-day Tishrei treat!

INGREDIENTS
1/2 c. butter*, softened,
   or margarine
1 1/2 c. brown sugar
2 eggs
1/3 c. water
1 c. mashed, cooked pumpkin
1/2 t. vanilla
1 2/3 c. flour
3/4 t. salt
1/2 t. nutmeg
1 t. baking soda
1/2 t. cinnamon
1/2 c. chopped walnuts (optional)
1/2 c. chopped dates

UTENSILS
electric/rotary beaters
measuring cups/spoons
liquid measuring cup
assorted mixing bowls
strainer
rubber scraper
muffin pan/s (for 12 muffins)
wooden spoon

❶ **Preheat** oven to 350°.

❷ **Cream** butter or margarine and brown sugar with beaters in medium bowl. **Add eggs. Beat** well. **Add** water, pumpkin, and vanilla and **beat** again.

❸ **Sift** dry ingredients through strainer into smaller bowl. **Mix** and **add** dry ingredients to pumpkin mixture. **Mix** thoroughly. **Fold in** walnuts and dates.

❹ **Pour** mixture into nonstick muffin pan cups and **bake** at 350° for 25–30 minutes or until tops are golden brown and a toothpick inserted in the middle comes out clean. Makes 12 medium muffins. Muffins can be frozen.

---

5 BOOKS OF TORAH
Q. Can you name all five books of the Torah, in order?

A. *B'reishit*—Genesis
Sh'mot—Exodus
Vayikra—Leviticus
Bamidbar—Numbers
D'varim—Deuteronomy

TORAH ROLLERS
Q. What is the name for the wooden rollers to which the Torah scroll is attached?

A. *Atzei chayim,* or "trees of life."

PROTECTING THE LETTERS
It is so important not to smudge the letters of the Torah that we use a pointer when we read from it, called a *yad,* or "hand." It is usually shaped like a small hand pointing its index finger.

TORAH CROWNS
In order to make the text of the Torah even more beautiful, certain letters have crowns added to them. The Torah itself can also have crowns, called *rimonim,* "pomegranates." They are usually worked in silver and have bells, like the pomegranate-shaped bells on the hem of the High Priest's garment in the Temple.

"Hi Ho Chanukah"—a whimsical look at Chanukah on the range.

Chanukah

Chanukah, the "Feast of Rededication" or the" Festival of Lights," celebrates the victory of a small band of Jews over the great Greco-Syrian army in 165 b.c.e. At that time, the Land of Israel was conquered by King Antiochus and his army. The Greeks brought with them many new things—libraries and theaters, gymnasiums and aqueducts, philosophy and religion—and they set up temples to their gods. Many Jews admired the Greeks and wanted to be more like them, but there were also Jews who resented the Greeks. Antiochus passed laws forbidding Jews to practice their religion. Suddenly, observing Shabbat, keeping kosher and studying Torah were against the law. Antiochus sent out soldiers to enforce his laws. The soldiers ransacked the Temple in Jerusalem. They replaced the beautiful, sacred objects with statues of their gods, and they forced the Jews to bow down to them. A Jewish man named Mattathias refused. He and his sons fled to the mountains and formed a rebel band, led by his son Judah. They called themselves "the Maccabees." Eventually more people joined them, and after many years, they miraculously defeated the mighty Greek army and took back their land. They cleaned up the Temple and rededicated it. According to tradition, when they went to light the menorah, they found only enough oil to last one day. Miraculously, the oil burned for eight days. To this day, we eat foods fried in oil—like potato latkes and jelly doughnuts—and we celebrate Chanukah for eight days and nights, to remind us of the miracles that happened so long ago.

KISLEV/November–December

Pareve

Lisa's Latkes

This is my great-grandmother's recipe, but since she didn't use measurements, I had to be creative. Feel free to experiment!

INGREDIENTS	UTENSILS
1 large onion	hand grater
4 medium potatoes, not peeled	spatula
	wooden spoon
1 egg	tablespoon
1 clove garlic, minced	measuring cups/spoons
1/2 t. salt	large mixing bowl
dash pepper	frying pan
1/4 t. garlic powder	baking sheet
1/4 cup matzah meal	paper towels/newspaper
oil for frying	

MAKING THE LATKE MIX

❶ **Peel** and **chop** onion. **Dump** into large mixing bowl.

❷ **Wash** potatoes and **cut off** all "eyes" and bad spots. Do not peel potatoes! (This will make the latkes crunchier and healthier.) Carefully **grate** potatoes by hand into a large mixing bowl, layering with onions. **Drain off** any excess liquid.

❸ **Crack** egg into bowl with potatoes and onion. **Add** minced garlic, salt, pepper, garlic powder, and matzah meal.

❹ **Mix** everything with a wooden spoon until well blended. Now you're ready to fry those latkes!

FRY 'EM UP IN A PAN (This is a job for an adult only!)

❶ **Turn on** the oven to **warm**.

❷ **Take out** a large frying pan or skillet, oil, and a spatula. **Turn** stove on **medium-high** and **pour** oil into pan. DO NOT POUR BATTER INTO PAN UNTIL OIL IS VERY HOT.

REMEMBER THE OIL
We traditionally eat fried foods on Chanukah to remind us of the oil that miraculously lasted for eight days in the newly rededicated Temple in Jerusalem.

For Ashkenazic Jews (Jews from Eastern Europe where potatoes were common), latkes, or potato pancakes, are a favorite dish on Chanukah.

In Israel, jelly doughnuts, or *sufganiot* are a popular Chanukah treat.

Sephardic Jews (Jews from Spain and Portugal) don't make latkes because they did not have potatoes in Spain until the sixteenth century, almost 100 years after the Jews had left Spain and Portugal because of the Inquisition.

Persian Jews enjoy *zelebi*, a snail-shaped, deep-fried dessert.

You can **test** the oil to see if it's hot enough by carefully dropping a tiny bit of latke mixture into the pan. When the mixture starts sizzling noisily and turning brown, the oil is ready for action!

❸ **Spoon** mixture into hot oil using a heaping tablespoon for measurement, and flatten slightly with a spatula.

❹ **Flip** latke over when edges start to get crisp. When both sides are golden brown, **remove** from pan and **drain** between sheets of paper towel (to absorb some of the oil). To save paper towel, you can use layers of newspaper with one paper towel on top and bottom (touching the latkes).

❺ **After draining** the latkes, **place** them in a single layer on a baking sheet and **put** in the oven to keep warm until all are ready. **Repeat** steps until all the mixture is used. **Serve** with Big Apple Applesauce and sour cream. Makes about 22 latkes.

TO FREEZE LATKES: Spread latkes singly on a baking sheet or tray and **put** in freezer. When individually frozen, **place** latkes in a plastic zip-top bag and **put back** in freezer.

TO SERVE: Arrange frozen latkes on baking sheet or tray and **heat** in 450° oven for about 7–10 minutes.

ISRAELI DREIDELS

Q. If the letters ש ה ג נ nun, gimel, hei and **shin** on the dreidel stand for "A great miracle happened **there**," what letters are on a dreidel from Israel?

A. פ ה ג נ nun, gimel, hei & **pey**, "A great miracle happened **here**."

Lucky latke leftovers enjoy a game of dreidel.

KISLEV/November–December

Pareve

Big Apple Applesauce

Comfort food from the "Big Apple"—New York City. On a cold winter's night, what better way to celebrate Chanukah than to curl up with a plate of steaming latkes and a large helping of this chunky, naturally sweetened side dish!

INGREDIENTS
5–6 apples, any kind*
water
about 1 t. cinnamon

UTENSILS
vegetable peeler
large saucepan
wooden spoon
potato masher or large fork
paring knife
cutting board

*I prefer Gala or Golden Delicious,
with a Granny Smith thrown in for extra zing!

❶ **Wash** and **peel** apples. **Cut** apples into quarters, **cut out** the cores, then **cut** each quarter into bite-size chunks. **Put** pieces in a large saucepan with a little water (about 1/3 cup).

❷ **Put** pot on stove and **turn on** medium-low heat. **Cook** apples, **stirring** often. Apples will cook down and become soft. When apples start to break down, **turn off** heat and use a potato masher or large fork to **smash** the remaining chunks into applesauce. **Add** more water until it is the thickness you like. **Add** cinnamon to taste. **Stir** well. Makes about 5 cups of chunky applesauce.

JOKE CORNER
Q. What do you call a black and white spotted spinning top?

A. *A Holstein dreidel!*

Q. In the days of the Wild West, what did they call the tiny potatoes who sat in the stands at the rodeo and cheered on their favorite Chanukah Candle Wrangler?

A. *Spec-tators!*

Q. What did they call the plain potato who announced the winner?

A. *Common-tator!*

LIGHTING THE CANDLES
To light the Chanukiah, the Chanukah menorah, the candles are put in from right to left and lit from left to right, with the newest candle lit first. In this way, light is increased so that on the darkest night of the holiday the light is the brightest. The candle we use to light all the other candles, the helper candle, is called the shamash.

KISLEV/November–December

Dairy* or Pareve

Maccabee Mushroom Burgers

The story of Chanukah is about fighting for religious freedom and independence despite impossible odds. May these healthy 100% vegetarian burgers give you the strength of Maccabees!

INGREDIENTS
3/4 c. finely minced walnuts
10 large mushrooms,** minced
1 stalk celery, minced
1 carrot, peeled and minced
1 small onion, finely minced
1–2 cloves garlic, minced
1 t. salt
1/8 t. black pepper
1 T. dry sherry (or any dry red wine)
1/2 t. dry mustard
1/2 c. rolled oats
1 c. water
1 T. *butter or oil + extra for frying patties
1/2 c. toasted (or raw) wheat germ (optional)

UTENSILS
spatula
large mixing bowl
cutting board & chopping knife or food processor
large frying pan
measuring cups/spoons
vegetable peeler
small saucepan
rubber scraper
wooden spoon

**You can also use 10 baby Portabellos or 1 1/4 huge Portabello mushrooms.

❶ **Mince** the walnuts, mushrooms, celery, carrot, onion, and garlic by hand or in a food processor and **place** in large mixing bowl. **Add** salt, pepper, sherry, and dry mustard and **mix** well.

❷ **Pour** mixture into a large frying pan and **sauté** in butter or oil over medium-low heat for about 10–15 minutes or until all ingredients are soft and tender, stirring often with a spatula. (While this is sautéing, you can do step 3.)

❸ **Measure** oats and water into a small saucepan and

bring to a boil over medium heat. **Turn down** temperature and **cook** for about 3 minutes or until thickened, **stirring** often. **Remove** from heat and add to mixture in pan. Add wheat germ (if desired) and mix well.

❹ **Transfer** mixture to a bowl and **chill** in refrigerator for about 1 hour before forming patties. When chilled, **form** into 4-inch burgers with your hands, and **fry** in butter or oil until brown on both sides or **broil** about 8 minutes on each side. Makes about 4–6 soft patties.

NOTE: Uncooked patties can be individually wrapped and frozen until ready to prepare.

KISLEV/November–December

Dairy* or pareve

Carrot Soup

This is the perfect complement to a Chanukah meal and a nice way to warm up on a chilly winter's day.

INGREDIENTS
Bouillon for 6 c. broth
6 c. water
4–5 large carrots, peeled
1 onion, chopped
2 T. butter* or margarine
pinch of sugar, salt, & pepper
   to taste
1/4 c. raw rice
fresh parsley for garnish

UTENSILS
medium & large soup pot
wooden spoon
measuring cup
liquid measuring cup
chopping knife
vegetable peeler
blender or food processor

❶ **Boil** 6 cups of water. When boiling, **add** bouillon. **Stir** until dissolved.

❷ **Slice** carrots thin. **Chop** onion. **Sauté** carrots and onions in butter or margarine with salt, pepper, and sugar. **Cook** 15 minutes until soft.

❸ **Add** rice and enough broth to cover. **Cook** until rice is done, about 20 minutes.

❹ **Puree** in blender. (This is a grown-up's job—the soup is very hot and difficult to transfer from pot to blender and back.) **Pour** soup back into pot and **add** the rest of the broth. **Add** water if necessary. **Serve** garnished with parsley.

MIRACLES
Q. Why do we place our *Chanukiah* (Chanukah menorah) in or near a window?

A. *To publicize the miracle.*

Q. Can you name all the different miracles associated with Chanukah?

A. 1) *The small Maccabean band miraculously defeating the huge, well-trained Greco-Syrian army.*
2) *The miracle that all the Jews in Antiochus' empire did not assimilate into Greek culture.*
3) *The flask of oil, only enough for one day but lasting for eight days.*

PLAYING DREIDEL
Do you know what all the letters on a dreidel stand for?
נ = player gets nothing
ג = player gets all
ה = player gets half
ש = player puts one in

Dreidels in Israel have slightly different letters, using פ *instead of* ש.
פ = *player puts one in*

I Think It's a Miracle That...

Something Special Our Family Does for Chanukah:

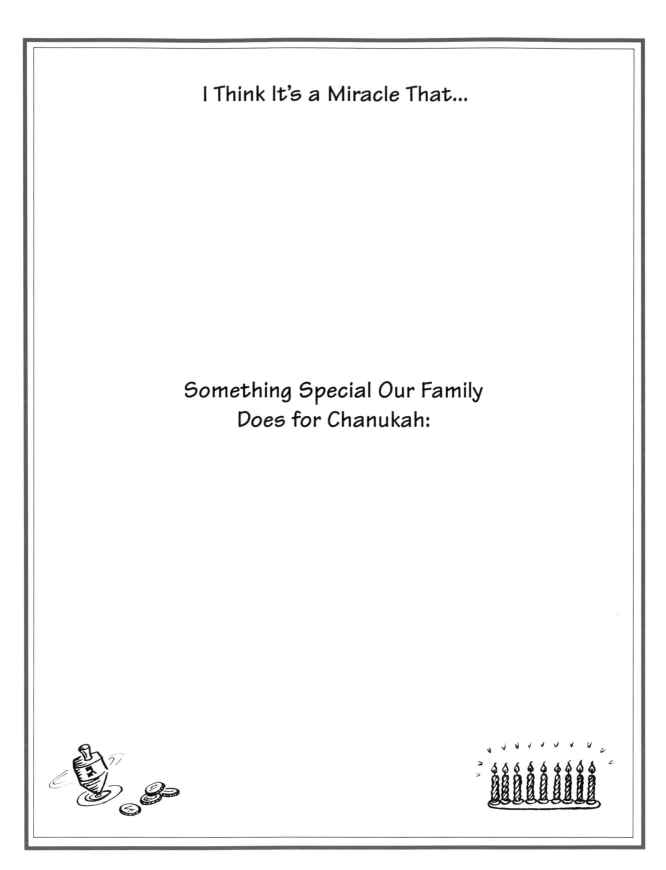

Veggies enjoying and planting trees on Tu Bishvat.

Tu Bishvat

Tu Bishvat is the "New Year of the Trees." Its name means the fifteenth day of the month of Shevat. On this holiday, we celebrate the beginning of spring in Israel. There trees are just beginning to show their new buds, even though in North America it is still winter. We celebrate Tu Bishvat by planting trees, here in our communities or in Israel. Trees are especially needed in Israel to make the desert land fertile and beautiful once again. Sometimes we give money so that other people can plant trees for us in the land of Israel. Trees have always been important in Judaism. The Torah itself is compared to a tree of life, nourishing us with the fruit of its wisdom. In fact, the wooden rollers holding the scroll together are called *atzei chayim,* literally "trees of life." In ancient times, when Jews would go to war and conquer a land, we were expressly forbidden to destroy any fruit-bearing trees belonging to our enemies, for that would prevent the people from having food to eat. And the Talmud teaches us that the words of Torah are like a fig tree. Why? Because unlike most trees, which only bear fruit at one time, whenever you search a fig tree, you can find figs ready to eat. So too with words of Torah: whenever you are engaged in studying them, you will find morsels of wisdom *(Babylonian Talmud Eruvin 54a,b).*

Shevat/January-February

Pareve

Nutty Fruit Salad

This refreshing salad can be made with almost any combination of your favorite fruits, so go wild! I have made some suggestions, but feel free to be creative!

INGREDIENTS
2 apples, any kind, chopped
1 orange, in sections
1/2 cantaloupe, cubed
1/2 honeydew , cubed
1 pear, chopped
juice of 1 orange
chopped walnuts or pecans
4–5 strawberries (or 1 c. of
    any other berries)
1–2 kiwis, peeled and sliced
1 banana, sliced
fresh mint (optional)

UTENSILS
large bowl
chopping knife
cutting board
juicer
vegetable peeler

❶ **Take out** a large bowl and **assemble** fruit. **Wash** all fruit. **Core** the apples and pear, and **cut** the rind off the melons. Now **cut up** apples, orange, melon, and pear into bite-size pieces. **Mix together**.

❷ **Squeeze** one orange with a juicer and **pour** the juice over the fruit pieces. This will help keep the fruit from turning brown and will add a little zing.

❸ **Add** the nuts to the salad and lightly **toss** to mix in. Walnuts can be **chopped.** but pecans can go in **whole**.

❹ Now **add** the berries. Most berries can go in **whole**, but strawberries can be **sliced**. If using kiwis and/or bananas, **peel** and **slice** and **add** to salad right before you serve it, so they won't turn brown.

❺ **Garnish** with fresh mint right before serving.

HOW TO MAKE A FRIENDSHIP FRUIT SALAD: Invite a group of friends over and **ask** each one **to bring** a different kind of fruit. When everyone arrives, **work together** to **cut** it up and **mix** it all together. Now you have a Friendship Salad! Enjoy the company and the food!

NEW FRUIT
On Tu Bishvat many people eat a fruit they haven't tasted since the year before. Before eating it, they say the blessing for that fruit and the Shehecheyanu, the blessing for doing something for the first time. Some people try to eat fifteen new fruits, in honor of the fifteenth of Shevat!

TU BISHVAT SEDER
The custom of holding a Tu Bishvat seder to study, taste, and celebrate the fruit of the tree, is increasing in popularity. The seder, like the Pesach seder, involves four cups of wine or juice, usually different colors or combinations, representing the different seasons of the year. With each cup, a different group of fruit is offered and tasted. Many divide the groups this way: (1) fruits edible on the inside but not on the outside (pomegranate, almond, orange), (2) those with inedible pits (olive, date, apple, avocado), and (3) those completely edible (seedless grapes, figs, raisins).

SHEVAT/January–February

Dairy

Chinese Almond Cookies

No Jewish cookbook would be complete without at least one Chinese recipe, and this one's a classic! These rich, chewy cookies go wonderfully with tea or milk.

INGREDIENTS
1 c. butter (2 sticks), room temperature
1/2 c. granulated sugar
1/4 c. firmly packed brown sugar
1 egg
1 t. almond extract
2 1/4 c. all-purpose flour
1/8 t. salt
1 1/2 t. baking powder
about 28 whole blanched almonds

FOR BASTING:
1 egg yolk
1 t. water

UTENSILS
assorted mixing bowls
sifter or strainer
beaters
rubber scraper
measuring cups/spoons
cookie sheets
wooden spoon
basting brush
spatula
table knife
pot holders
wire rack

❶ **Preheat** oven to 350°.

❷ **Cream** butter, granulated sugar, and brown sugar until fluffy. **Add** egg and almond extract and **beat** until well blended. You might have to use a knife to get the batter off the beaters partway; the dough can get a little sticky.

❸ **Sift** flour, salt, and baking powder into a smaller bowl. **Add** to creamed mixture and **blend** well with the beaters or a wooden spoon.

❹ To shape each cookie, **roll** 1 tablespoon of dough at a time **into a ball** with your hands. **Place** balls of dough 2 inches apart on an ungreased cookie sheet, and **flatten**

WHY ALMONDS?
It is customary to eat foods with almonds on Tu Bishvat. Why? Because almond trees are the first trees to flower in the Land of Israel.

THE SEVEN SPECIES
By the fifteenth of Shevat, the Land of Israel is blooming, the winter rains are almost over, and it is time to enjoy the fruit of the soil, especially the seven species for which Israel is praised: grapes, figs, pomegranates, dates (date honey), olives (olive oil), wheat, and barley.

NEW YEAR FOR TREES
Q. Tu Bishvat is the "New Year for the Trees." But there are four New Years in the Jewish calendar. Can you name the other three?

A. 1) First of Tishrei— Rosh Hashanah—New Year for the Counting of Years

2) First of Nisan—New Year for Kings and Festivals

3) First of Elul—New Year for Animals

very slightly with the palm of your hand. **Press** an almond into the center of each round.

❺ **Beat** egg yolk and 1 teaspoon water in a small bowl.
Brush a little on each cookie with a pastry brush. This will
make the cookies shiny.

❻ **Bake** at 350° for 10–15 minutes or until lightly brown
at the edges, but still pale. **Remove** from sheets with a
spatula and **cool** on wire racks. Makes about 24 cookies.
Store in an airtight container.

What I Can Do to Help the Earth:

What I Like Most about Trees:

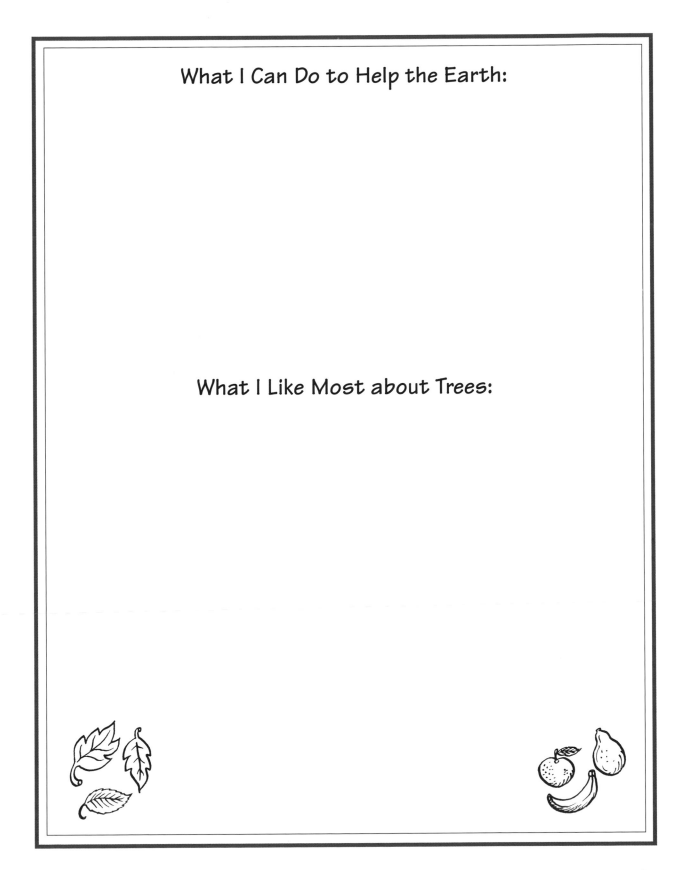

Chai, Hadassah, and Harry Hashuerus Hamantashen living it up in Shushan.

Purim

Purim is the holiday that celebrates our people's escape from destruction at the hands of evil Haman, prime minister to King Ahashuerus of ancient Persia. Haman wanted to kill the Jews because they would not bow down to him, and if it were not for brave Queen Esther and her uncle Mordechai, Haman would have succeeded. Purim means "lots" and is so named because Haman drew lots to determine on which day the Jews would be killed. The story is handwritten on a scroll similar to a Torah scroll but with only one roller, called a *megillah*, or the Scroll of Esther. The holiday of Purim, which falls on the fourteenth day of the month of Adar, is one of the only holidays in the Jewish calendar that expressly commands us to be happy. And nothing makes people happier than cookies! It is traditional to bake triangular shaped cookies, called hamantashen, reminiscent of Haman's three-cornered hat (or some say ears), and deliver them to friends and relatives during this time. What better way to enjoy the holiday than to witness the look of surprise and joy on someone's face when you present them with a basket of these freshly baked goodies! Be happy, it's Adar!

ADAR/February–March

Dairy* or Pareve

Prize-Winning Hamantashen

These hamantashen won first prize for the best tasting dough and filling. The recipe for the filling originally comes from Hadassah Magazine, 1980, but the source of the dough remains a mystery. With a twist on the traditional prune, poppy seed, or fruit filling, these hamantashen are a delicious blend of many different tastes and can be made in advance and frozen, or eaten hot out of the oven! Enjoy!

NOTE: This recipe can be made dairy or pareve. For dairy, use butter and milk; for pareve, substitute pareve margarine and water or soy/rice milk. All versions are delicious!

INGREDIENTS
FILLING:
1 c. finely ground walnuts
$7/8$ c. sugar
$1/2$ t. vanilla
juice of half a lemon
juice of half an orange
4 figs, finely chopped
$2^1/2$ oz. dates (about 6), finely chopped
$1/4$ c. butter* or margarine, melted
$1/4$ c. raisins
$1/2$ t. cinnamon
$1/4$ c. apricot jam
1 T. rum

DOUGH:
1 c. butter* or margarine
$1^1/2$ c. sugar
2 eggs
4 c. flour
4 t. baking powder
2 T. milk*, water, or soy/rice milk
2 t. vanilla

UTENSILS
assorted mixing bowls
tablespoon
wooden spoon
rolling pin
measuring cups/spoons
spatula
juicer
electric beaters
cookie sheets
3-4" round cookie cutter or drinking glass
wire cooling rack
dough blender
food processor

MAKING THE FILLING

❶ **Take out** a large mixing bowl. **Measure** the walnuts, sugar, and vanilla and **pour** into the bowl.

❷ Using a juicer, **squeeze** the juice of half a lemon and half an orange. **Pour** the juice into the bowl with the nuts and sugar.

❸ **Chop** the figs and dates into small pieces. **Add** to bowl.

❹ **Melt** the butter (or margarine) either in a microwave-safe dish in the microwave or in a small pot on the stove. **Pour** into bowl.

❺ **Measure** and **add** raisins, cinnamon, jam, and rum. **Combine** all ingredients and **mix** well with a wooden spoon.

MAKING THE DOUGH

❶ In a large mixing bowl, **cream** together butter (or margarine) and sugar with beaters. **Add** eggs and **beat** a little more.

❷ In a smaller bowl, **mix** flour and baking powder. **Add** a little of this mixture to the creamed butter, sugar, and egg.

❸ **Add** the milk (regular, rice, or soy) to the creamed mixture. **Add** the remaining flour mixture. **Add** the vanilla. **Mix** well.

FORMING THE HAMANTASHEN

❶ **Preheat** oven to 375°. **Knead** the cookie dough into a ball and **roll out** on a floured board until $1/8$ to $1/4$-inch thick.

❷ **Cut** dough into 3 to 4-inch rounds with a floured glass or cookie cutter.

❸ **Drop** filling by teaspoon in the center of each round.

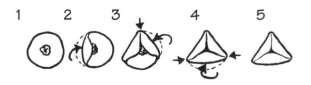

ON HIDING
On Purim, Jews all over the world eat foods filled with sweet fruits or meat and hidden by a layer of dough. Ashkenazic Jews eat *hamantashen* filled with poppy seed or other fruit filling; Persian, Iraqi, and Indian Jews eat *sambusak*, stuffed with dates or chicken; Romanian Jews make *beigli*, yeast-dough cookies that look like children wrapped (hidden) in blankets. All of these symbolize the special hidden miracles of Purim. They also remind us that Esther hid her true identity in order to survive in the palace and of the courage she showed when she ceased her hiding and stood up for who she was.

❹ **Pinch together** sides of circle to form a triangle. **Pinch** the corners **tightly**, or cookies will come apart when baked.

❺ **Place** cookies on a lightly greased cookie sheet. **Leave** a little **space** around each one, so they have room to rise. When cookie sheet is full, carefully **put** it in the oven. If you have another cookie sheet, you can get another batch ready while the first is baking, or fill two and then put them into the oven together.

❻ **Bake** at 375° for 15–25 minutes. When they are lightly browned, they are done. If the dough is still very white, bake them 2 minutes more.

❼ **Carefully remove** trays from the oven using a pot holder. **Lift** cookies off with a spatula and **place** them on a wire rack to cool. Makes about 4 dozen.

ADAR/February–March

Dairy

Vermicelli Cheese Pudding

This recipe comes from my friend Leora Troper's grandmother, Janet Miller, in England. It is based on a recipe she got from the British government during World War II, when there was a campaign in England to teach people how to make food (in this case, eggs) go further during the time of food rationing. It has been modified through the years by family members and was passed on to me a few years ago—a true family folk recipe. It is a wonderful, easy dish to bring to someone's house for a Purim potluck, and it tastes great, too!

INGREDIENTS
water for boiling
10-12 oz. coiled vermicelli
6-8 oz. cheese (mostly
    cheddar, with Muenster,
    Gouda or Monterey Jack)
2 eggs
1/2 t. salt
pepper to taste
1 t. sweet basil
1/4 t. garlic powder
1/4 t. onion powder (optional)
1 can peeled, diced
    tomatoes (about 14-16 oz.,
    with or without spices)
margarine, butter, or
    cooking spray

UTENSILS
13 x 9-inch baking dish
hand grater
large & small mixing bowls
rubber scraper
wooden spoon
medium saucepan
colander
fork
can opener
pot holders

❶ **Preheat** oven to 350°.

❷ **Fill** a saucepan with water and put on the stove at medium-high heat. When water is boiling, **add** vermicelli noodles and **cook** according to package directions. When noodles are done, **drain** in colander.

❸ While water is boiling, **grate** cheese. **Beat** eggs with a fork in a small bowl. **Mix in** spices. **Add** tomatoes to egg mixture. (You can drain the tomatoes first, but I prefer to use the tomato juice.)

❹ **Add** cooked noodles to large mixing bowl. Gradually **add** grated cheese and **mix in** evenly. Now **add** tomato-egg mixture. **Mix** well.

❺ *Grease* baking dish. **Pour** everything into the dish and **bake** at 350° for 45 minutes to 1 hour, or until top starts to get crispy. Serves 10–12.

Dairy* or Pareve

Mom's Chocolate Chip Cookie Mix

What would a cookbook be without a recipe for chocolate chip cookies?! What makes these special? You can mix all the dry ingredients ahead of time and put the mix in the refrigerator or freezer until you're ready to make cookies. Then all you need to do is add eggs and vanilla and you're ready to bake! And it's all natural ingredients. They also make a nice addition to a shalach manot basket for Purim.

INGREDIENTS
(for 2 batches of mix)
4 1/2 c. flour
2 t. baking soda
1 t. salt
1 1/2 c. granulated sugar
1 1/2 c. firmly packed brown sugar
2 c. unsalted butter* or margarine**
2 c. chopped walnuts (optional)
2 pkg. (12 oz. each) chocolate chips

FOR ONE BATCH:
2 eggs
1 t. vanilla
7 cups of mix

***I have made these with margarine, but butter works much better.*

UTENSILS
large mixing bowl
fork
dough blender or knife
wooden spoon
airtight container or zip-top freezer bags
cookie sheets
2 teaspoons
wire racks
pot holders
spatula
measuring cups/spoons

MAKING THE MIX
❶ **Combine** flour, baking soda, salt, and sugars in large bowl.
❷ **Cut in** butter with a dough blender or table knife until crumbly.

QUEEN VASHTI
Queen Esther deserves a lot of credit for her courage in risking her life and standing up to the king, but what about Vashti, King Ahashuerus's first wife? Her bravery tends to be forgotten. Legend has it that Vashti was a strong, independent woman, and when asked by the (very tipsy) king to come before him wearing only her crown, she flatly refused. The king was very angry that she did not obey him. His advisors were afraid that if the women in the town heard about Vashti's standing up to her husband, there would be chaos and all women would no longer obey their husbands. So the king sent Vashti away and went looking for a new wife, one who he hoped would be more submissive. And he got Esther. The rest is history!

❸ **Stir in** nuts (if desired) and chocolate chips. **Store** mix in an airtight container or in zip-top freezer bags in the refrigerator or freezer until ready to use.

FOR ONE BATCH OF COOKIES
❹ **Preheat** oven to 375°. **Grease** cookie sheets. **Beat** 2 eggs slightly with a fork in a large bowl. **Add** 1 teaspoon vanilla and 7 cups of the cookie mix. **Mix** until well blended.

❺ **Drop** dough by heaping teaspoon onto greased cookie sheets. **Bake** in preheated oven at 375° for about 8–10 minutes or until golden brown. **Remove** with spatula and **cool** on wire racks. One batch makes about 60 cookies.

HAMAN'S KIDS
Q. How do we read the names of Haman's ten sons in the megillah?

A. All in one breath so that not more than one breath is wasted on them.

My Favorite Thing about Purim:

Things We Can Put in Our
Shalach Manot Packages:

B'chol dor vador—"In every generation"...
each ingredient should feel as though it personally went forth from Egypt.

Pesach

When new leaves appear on the trees and flowers start poking through the snow, it must be time for Pesach! Pesach is the holiday of rebirth, of spring, of freedom and of matzah. It is a week-long festival commemorating the Israelite's Exodus from Egypt and the beginning of political freedom for a people who had been slaves for 400 years. The Hebrew word *pasach* means "passing over." When God sent the ten plagues on the Egyptians to pressure Pharaoh to free the Israelites, God passed over the Hebrews so we call this holiday Pesach, or Passover. Pesach is centered around a ceremonial meal called the *seder*. The *seder* can be traditional or very creative, but it always requires organization; we ask specific questions, tell the story of our Exodus, eat special foods, and sing songs, all in a specific order. The word *seder* means "order," and the book we use to tell the story and keep everything in order is called the *haggadah*. When the Hebrews left Egypt, they were in such a hurry that the dough they had prepared to make bread for the journey had no time to rise, so they carried it on their backs until they could bake it. Because it couldn't rise properly, the bread was flat and dry. Every year at Pesach we still eat this "bread of affliction," or matzah, and we eat no foods made with grain or leavening, or *chametz*. We clean our homes extra carefully to get rid of any trace of *chametz*. When everything is clean and prepared, we are finally ready for Pesach. Here are some traditional and not-so-traditional Pesach edibles. And all are kosher for Pesach. Enjoy!

NISAN/March–April

Pareve

Multi-Cultural Charoset

Charoset was always my favorite part of the Passover seder; it even has its own spot on the seder plate. Charoset symbolizes both our slavery and our freedom and is made in many different ways. This recipe blends two traditions. It is a chunky combination of the traditional apple, nuts, and cinnamon style charoset of Ashkenazic Jews and the raisin, date, and orange medley of the Sephardic tradition. Enjoy the sweet taste of freedom and experience two cultures in one!

INGREDIENTS
3 apples, peeled & cored
juice of 1 orange
juice of half a lemon
1 1/2 c. walnuts, chopped
approx. 12 dates
approx. 6 figs
1/4 c. raisins
2 1/2 T. sweet red wine
1 t. cinnamon
1 t. vanilla

UTENSILS
food processor and/or
    chopper & bowl
wooden spoon
chopping knife
measuring spoons & cups
large mixing bowl
large cutting board
hand juicer

❶ **Peel** and **core** apples. **Chop** in food processor or by hand, using either a chopping bowl and chopper (my favorite) or a cutting board and sharp knife. **Chop** apples into small pieces, about the size of corn kernels. **Put** into large bowl.

❷ **Squeeze** the juice of 1 orange and half of a lemon with a hand juicer, and **pour** into bowl over apples. **Add** chopped nuts.

❸ **Chop** dates and figs by hand and **add** to bowl. (Dates and figs are difficult to chop in a food processor.) Be sure to **remove** any pits or hard stems. **Add** raisins.

❹ Now **add** wine, cinnamon, and vanilla and **mix** well with a wooden spoon. **Taste** to make sure you like it! **Add** a little more wine, cinnamon, or orange juice, if necessary, until it's just right! Makes about 5 cups.

Charoset can be kept in the refrigerator for at least a week. Have it with plain or vanilla yogurt for a yummy, healthy snack!

NISAN/March–April

Dairy

Spinach Cheese Patties/Kugel*

These tasty, filling treats might have been what gave the ancient Hebrews the strength to continue wandering for forty years. Who knows, maybe they continued wandering so they could keep enjoying these treats! You decide!

INGREDIENTS
1 (10 oz.) box chopped, frozen spinach
1 carrot, grated
1/2 onion, chopped fine
1/2 c. matzah meal
2 eggs
4 T. Feta or Bulgarian cheese
2 T. (light or regular) cream cheese
salt, pepper, onion & garlic powder, to taste
butter, margarine, or cooking spray

UTENSILS
wooden spoon
large mixing bowl
measuring cups/spoons
spatula/rubber scraper
chopping knife
hand grater

FOR PATTIES:
baking sheet*

FOR KUGEL:
baking pan or baking dish

*You can make this either as separate patties or in a baking dish as a kugel. Either way, the first step is the same. Recipe can be doubled.

FOR BOTH PATTIES AND KUGEL
❶ **Defrost** spinach. **Drain** liquid. **Mix together** all ingredients in a large mixing bowl.

FOR PATTIES
❷ **Form** into patties about 1/2 inch thick and 2 1/2 inches in diameter.

❸ **Place** patties on a lightly greased baking sheet. **Bake** in 375° oven for 5-7 minutes on each side, until lightly brown on both sides. Makes approximately 8 patties.

FOR KUGEL

❷ Preheat oven to 375° (350° for glass). **Spread** kugel mixture evenly in a lightly greased 8x8x2-inch pan or baking dish. **Bake** until top is lightly brown and center is firm, about 30 minutes.**

❸ Cool on wire rack and then **cut** into squares.

**NOTE: When kugel recipe is doubled, it fits into a 13 x 9 x 2-inch baking pan and bakes for 30 minutes.

Marvelous Macaroons

This recipe is easy, delicious, and always leaves them wanting more! Make them chocolate, vanilla or almond, for a tasty seder dessert that will make them think you slaved all day!

INGREDIENTS
2/3 c. sweetened condensed milk(regular or low-fat)
3 c. shredded sweetened coconut
1 t. vanilla (or almond extract)

FOR CHOCOLATE MACAROONS
1 oz. square unsweetened baking chocolate, melted

UTENSILS
medium mixing bowl
mixing spoon
measuring cups & spoons
1–2 cookie sheets
2 teaspoons
rubber scraper
spatula
wire cooling racks
small microwave-safe bowl
pot holders
kitchen parchment paper

❶ **Preheat** oven to 350°. Line cookie sheets with parchment paper.

FOR ALMOND MACAROONS
❷ **Combine** all ingredients in mixing bowl, **using almond extract**. **Continue** to step 3.

FOR CHOCOLATE AND VANILLA MACAROONS
❷ **Combine** all ingredients in mixing bowl, **using vanilla extract**. FOR VANILLA macaroons, go to step 3 now. FOR CHOCOLATE macaroons, **melt** baking chocolate in small bowl in microwave until just softened, but not completely melted. **Stir** with a spoon until chocolate is completely melted. **Add** to larger bowl using a rubber scraper. **Mix**.

FOR ALL
❸ **Use** teaspoons **to drop** heaping spoonfuls of mixture about 1 inch apart on lined baking sheets. (The parchment paper will keep the macaroons from sticking.)

SEDER PLATE SYMBOLS
Q. What items are on the seder plate?

A. **1)** Charoset—sweet mixture of apples, nuts, and cinnamon (or other sweet dried fruit and spices)
2) Maror—bitter herb, usually horseradish
3) Pesach—a roasted shank bone, or at vegetarian seders, a roasted beet
4) Betzah—a roasted egg
5) Karpas—a green vegetable, usually parsley
6) Chatzeret—the bitter core of Romaine lettuce
7) An orange—used by some people as a new symbol of the importance of women in Jewish life

SAVING A PLACE
There is a custom of leaving an empty chair at the seder table, because of the direction to "let all who are hungry come and share the Pesach with us."

❹ **Bake** in preheated 350° oven for 10–15 minutes, or until edges are slightly browned. **Remove** carefully from the oven with a pot holder.

❺ **Let** macaroons **cool** slightly (a minute or two) and **remove** from baking sheets with a spatula or your fingers. **Place** on wire racks to cool. Makes about 24 macaroons. **Store** in a cookie tin or glass jar.

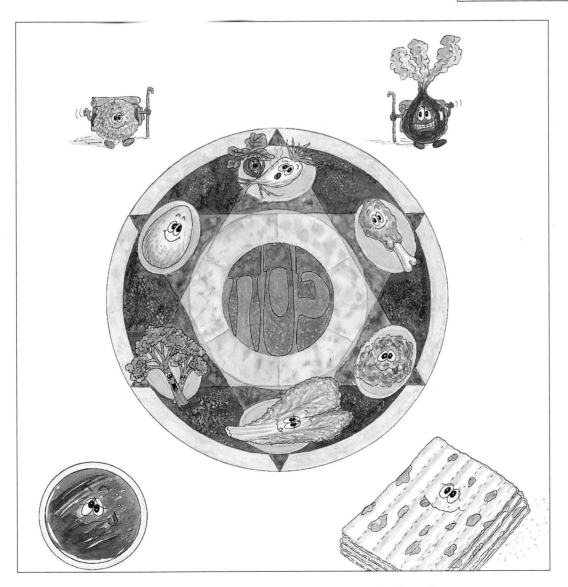

Pesach seder symbols, with new arrivals Ora Orange and Benjamin Beet, ready to celebrate freedom.

Exodus Veggie Stew

Just like the ingredients going out of Egypt, each one of us should feel as if we too experienced redemption. Each of us plays a unique role in our people's future. In our infinite diversity we are one. Savor the different tastes and textures in this medley of flavors, and let the experience set you free!

INGREDIENTS
1 onion, chopped
2 cloves garlic, pressed
3–4 medium carrots, peeled
   & sliced
3 medium stalks celery, diced
1 potato, peeled and chopped
1 T. fresh parsley, chopped
2 T. cooking sherry
2 T. honey
2 c. pareve chicken flavored
   stock
1 T. olive oil
1 bottle (10 oz.) tomato juice and
   3 small tomatoes, diced
      or
1 can diced tomatoes (with or
   without spices) in juice
1 can of beans, black or red, drained
   (optional)
2 medium zucchini, sliced (or other
   squash-type vegetable)
1 pkg. frozen peas (optional)
salt & pepper to taste

UTENSILS
cutting board
chopping knife
vegetable peeler
spatula
large pot with lid
can opener
wooden spoon
measuring spoons
measuring cup

❶ **Peel** and **chop** all ingredients.

❷ **Add** oil to pot and **turn on** medium heat. When oil is hot, **add** onions and celery. **Stir** with spatula, **cover**, and **cook** for 3 minutes. **Uncover, add** parsley, garlic, and carrots, **stir**, and cover for another 3 minutes.

DIFFERENT NAMES
Like many Jewish holidays, Pesach has many names:
1) *Chag ha-Aviv*— "Festival of Spring"
2) *Z'man Cheiruteinu*— "Time of Our Freedom"
3) *Chag ha-Matzot*— "Festival of Matzah"

FOR THE SAKE OF RIGHTEOUS WOMEN
Q. Who was responsible for saving Moses' life after Pharaoh decreed all Hebrew boys be thrown in the Nile?

A. 1) *Yocheved*, Moses' mother, who made a basket for him and set him afloat on the Nile.
2) *Pharaoh's daughter*, who found Moses and adopted him as her own son.
3) *Miriam*, Moses' sister, who watched over him and arranged for Yocheved to nurse young Moses.

Q. Who else challenged Pharaoh's authority and enabled more Hebrew children to live?

A. The midwives *Shifra* and *Pua*.

❸ **Add** rest of ingredients except peas to pot. **Stir** with wooden spoon. **Bring to a boil**, then **turn down** to medium-low and **simmer** uncovered, **stirring** occasionally, until potatoes and carrots are tender and liquid is mostly absorbed (about 2 hours).

❹ **Add** peas and **cook** about 5 minutes longer.

NOTE: Some Ashkenazic Jews do not eat legumes (peas and beans) on Passover. But Sephardic Jews and some vegetarians do.

For their civil disobedience and their courage, the great commentator Rashi states, "For the sake of righteous women, we were delivered from Egypt."
—B. Talmud Pesachim 108b

NISAN/March–April

Pareve

Chocolate Chip Freedom Brownies

These sinfully delicious kosher for Passover brownies are so rich and chocolaty you will want to eat them all year round. And you can! During the year, just substitute flour for matzah cake meal and add baking powder instead of baking soda. Enjoy your freedom to indulge!

INGREDIENTS
3/4 c. matzah cake meal*
1/8 t. baking soda**
1/2 t. salt
1 c. sugar
2 squares unsweetened
   baking chocolate
1/2 c. vegetable oil
2 eggs
1 t. vanilla
1/2 c. chopped walnuts
   (optional)
6 oz. kosher for Passover
   semisweet chocolate
   chips
margarine or nonstick
   cooking spray for pan

UTENSILS
8x8x2-inch baking pan
medium mixing bowl
wooden spoon
rubber scraper
measuring cups/spoons
liquid measuring cup
strainer
microwave-safe bowl
teaspoon
wire racks

FOR NON-PASSOVER
BAKING:
*3/4 c. flour
**1/2 t. baking powder

❶ **Preheat** oven to 350° (325° for glass pan). **Grease** baking pan.

❷ **Sift together** cake meal, baking soda, and salt in mixing bowl. **Add** sugar. DO NOT STIR YET.

❸ **Melt** chocolate in microwave-safe bowl until almost melted. **Remove** from microwave and **stir** until completely melted and smooth.

❹ **Pour** oil, eggs, vanilla, and melted chocolate into the center of the dry ingredients. **Stir** with a wooden spoon, slowly at first and then faster, **beating** until smooth.

CROSSING THE SEA

There is a *midrash*, a story, about the Exodus from Egypt that tells the tale of Nachshon ben Aminadav. When the waters of the Red Sea did not part immediately for the Israelites, Nachshon took a leap of faith and was the first to step into the waves. And it was only when the water was about to cover his head that the sea parted.

Some Jews explain that when we recite the *Mi Chamocha* prayer (the song Israel sang at the shores of the sea), we sing first "Mi **Chamocha**" and then "Mi **Kamocha**", tightening our throats at the second line as if we were Nachshon stepping into deep water and trying to keep from swallowing the sea.

Q. Who led the people in dancing and song at the shores of the Red Sea?

A. *Miriam.*

Mix in the nuts and chocolate chips. The oil will cause the batter to come away from the sides of the bowl.

❺ **Spread** batter evenly into the greased pan, **pushing** the batter into all the corners with a rubber scraper. **Bake** for about 25–30 minutes. Batter will smooth out in the oven and rise slightly. When a toothpick inserted in the center comes out mostly clean, **remove** from oven. DO NOT OVERBAKE. **Cool** on wire rack for about 15–18 minutes. **Cut** into squares and eat, or **cool completely** and **wrap** uncut brownies in foil and zip-top bags **to freeze**. Makes about 16 fudgy brownies.

Favorite Family Pesach Recipes:

Special Family Seder Traditions:

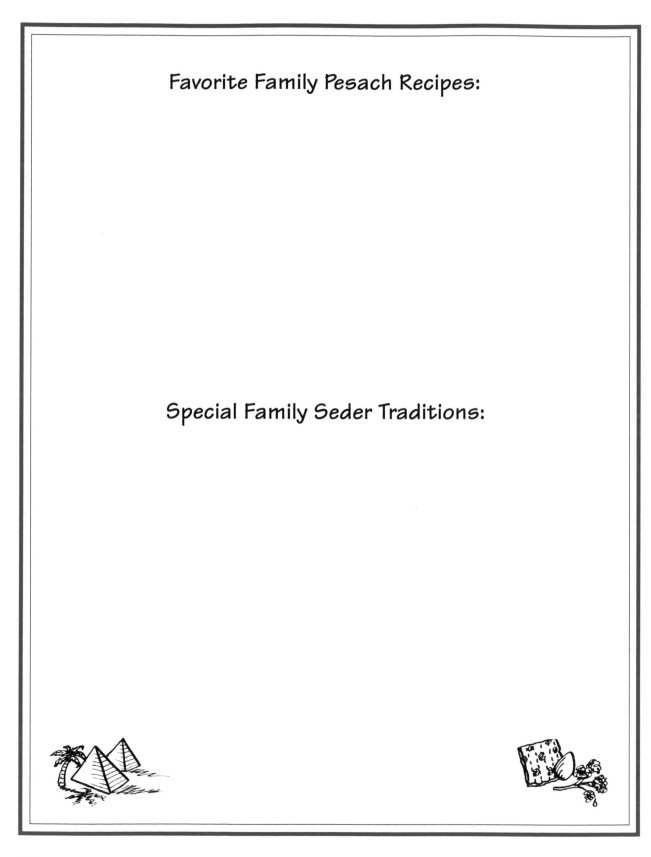

The seven species—Peninah Pomegranate, Olie & Olga Olive, Dani & Daffi Date, Wally Wheat, Benjie Barley, Gadi Grape, and Jaffa the Fig—out on the kibbutz.

Yom haAtzmaut

Yom ha Atzmaut is Israeli Independence Day. It is the day Jews celebrate regaining our independence and becoming a free people in the land of Israel. For the first time in two thousand years, the Jewish people have a homeland. The United Nations voted to create a Jewish state on November 29, 1947, and on May 14, 1948, the State of Israel was born. The day before Yom haAtzmaut we observe Yom haZikaron, Remembrance Day, when we remember all those who died to build and protect the country. In Israel on Yom haZikaron, a siren is sounded throughout the country, and when the siren starts, the whole country comes to a halt. People immediately stop and stand still, cars and buses stop and their drivers get out of their vehicles and stand in silence to remember the brave people who fell in Israel's wars. But on Yom haAtzmaut, we celebrate by dancing, waving flags, and singing Jewish songs. On this day, Jews all over the world celebrate with picnics and barbeques and Israeli foods like felafel and Israeli salad. Although bagels are a somewhat new delicacy in Israel, I have included them here, because what would a Jewish celebration be without them? Happy Independence Day!

IYAR/April–May

Pareve

Israeli Salad

There is nothing to compare to an Israeli tomato . . . there is just something about them that makes me wax poetic! Unlike most store-bought varieties in the United States, Israeli tomatoes taste like tomatoes! Even without Israeli tomatoes, this dish comes close to simulating the traditional staple of the Israeli table. It is the perfect dish for an outdoor lunch at your favorite picnic spot or to whip up for Shabbat lunch. It's easy and colorful and has all the tastes of summer in Israel!

INGREDIENTS	UTENSILS
1 cucumber (seedless is best)	chopping knife
2–3 Roma tomatoes	cutting board
juice of 1/2 lime*	medium bowl
1 T. fresh parsley	small strainer
	vegetable peeler

Lemon can be used if limes are not available.

❶ **Peel** cucumber (if not organic) and finely **dice**. **Dice** tomatoes. **Transfer** both to medium bowl. (There should be about the same amount of tomatoes as cucumbers.) **Add** more of either one as necessary.

❷ **Cut** a lime in half. **Take** one half and holding it over a small strainer so you don't get seeds in the salad, **squeeze** a little bit of juice over the salad. **Mix** the salad and then **squeeze** the rest of the juice from that half over the salad mixture.

❸ Finely **chop** fresh parsley and **sprinkle** over the salad. **Mix in** evenly. Can be kept refrigerated in an airtight container for a few days.

IYAR/April–May

Dairy or pareve

Bodacious Bagels

This recipe makes a bagel minyan (a prayer quorum of ten) and unlike some minyanim, this one is open and accepting of all types and flavors!

INGREDIENTS
3$^{1}/_{2}$ c. flour + extra for kneading
2 pkgs. dry yeast
3 T. sugar
$^{1}/_{2}$ T. salt
1$^{1}/_{2}$ c. hot water (120° -130°)
$^{1}/_{2}$ t. oil (for bowl)
margarine
cornmeal
3 qt. water

DUNKING:
3 qt. water
1$^{1}/_{2}$ T. malt syrup or sugar

BASTING:
1 egg white, beaten
1 t. water

toppings:
sesame seeds, poppy seeds, dried minced onion,
dried minced garlic, caraway seeds, Kosher salt, cinnamon

UTENSILS
2 baking sheets
spatula
wooden spoon
rubber scraper
assorted mixing bowls
wax paper
easuring cups & spoons
4$^{1}/_{2}$-quart saucepan
large skimmer
pastry brush
cooking thermometer
dish towel
wire cooling rack

MAKING THE DOUGH
❶ **Measure** 3 cups flour into a large mixing bowl. **Heat** 1$^{1}/_{2}$ cups water in microwave for about 2 minutes, until water is between 120°-130°. **Add** the dry yeast, sugar, and salt. **Pour** in the hot water and **stir** for 2 minutes. **Add** the rest of the flour ($^{1}/_{2}$ c.) a little bit at a time. **Stir** until dough gets thick and heavy. **Add** extra flour if the dough sticks to the sides of the bowl. **Remove** dough from bowl and **place** on floured work surface.

❷ **Knead** the dough for about 10 minutes, using the palm of your hand in a strong rhythm of **push-fold-turn**. Add

MORE ISRAEL TRIVIA
Q. The city of Jerusalem has a law that all buildings must be built with Jerusalem stone. What kind of stone is it?

A. *Limestone.*

At sunset and sunrise in Jerusalem, the light reflects off the Jerusalem stone of the city, and everything looks golden. That is why they call the city *Yerushalayim Shel Zahav,* or "Jerusalem of Gold."

Q. What is the name of Israel's national anthem, and what does it mean?

A. *"Hatikvah," meaning "The Hope" —the hope of "being a free people in our land, the land of Zion and Jerusalem."*

DID YOU KNOW . . .
In downtown Tel Aviv, there is a major street of shops and restaurants, called Dizengoff Street, named after the first mayor of the city. It is such a popular place that there is actually a word in Hebrew *l'hizdangef,* which means "to walk down Dizengoff."

flour if dough is sticky or elastic. Bagel dough should be firm and solid when you pinch it with your fingers.

❸ **Rub** 1/2 t. oil on the inside of a large mixing bowl. **Form** the dough into a round bundle and **transfer** to the oiled bowl. **Cover** with a clean dish towel and **set aside** at room temperature (or in an electric oven TURNED OFF with the light on) until doubled in bulk, about 1 hour. (If you are using fast-rising yeast at the recommended higher temperatures, **reduce** rising times by half.)

❹ While the dough is rising, **prepare** the baking sheets. **Rub** sheets with margarine and **sprinkle** with cornmeal, **turning** the sheets so that the meal sticks to the margarine and **covers** the whole sheet. Now **bring** 3 quarts of water **to a boil** in a large saucepan. When boiling, **add** malt syrup or sugar. **Reduce heat** and l**eave to simmer**—water should be barely moving.

❺ When dough has risen, **turn** dough onto a flat work surface and **punch down** with extended fingers. **Divide** the dough into 10 equal pieces. **Make** individually flavored bagels by **pressing** toppings into the dough with your fingers (i.e., for cinnamon raisin, add raisins and cinnamon, for rye, add caraway seeds, for onion, add some dried minced onion, etc.).

❻ Now **shape** each piece of dough into a ball. **Let** them **relax** for a few minutes before gently **flattening** them with the palm of your hand. Now with your thumb, **push through** the center of each and **pull open** a hole with your fingers. **Pull** the dough down over a finger and **smooth** the rough edges. Does it look like a bagel? (Make sure the holes are big enough—the dough will expand in the oven and the holes will close up if they are too small.)

❼ **Place** all 10 together on the work surface and **cover** with wax paper. **Leave** at room temperature until dough is slightly raised, about 10 minutes. (This is what professional bakers call "half-proofed.")

❽ **Preheat** oven to 400°. **Spread** a clean dish towel on the counter near the hot water. The water should be simmering. (The sugar in the water will make the dipped bagels shiny). **Gently lift** one bagel at a time using a large skimmer and **lower** into the hot water. Don't try to do more than 2 or 3 at a time. They don't like to be crowded! Ideally the bagels should sink and rise again after a few seconds. (If they don't sink, it's OK.) **Simmer** for $1/2$ minute on one side, then **gently flip** it over for another $1/2$ minute—1 minute total for each bagel. **Lift** each out with skimmer and **drain briefly** on the towel, then **transfer** to the prepared baking sheet. **Repeat** steps for all 10 bagels.

❾ Now is your chance to be creative with toppings! **Create** your own unique minyan! **Brush** bagels lightly with 1 egg white mixed with 1 teaspoon water and then **sprinkle** with any combination of toppings: poppy seed, sesame seed, minced onion, minced garlic, kosher salt (large crystals), caraway seed, cinnnamon, etc.

❿ Place baking sheets on the middle oven rack and **bake** at 425° for 25–30 minutes total. When tops are just light brown, **turn** them over and **finish baking**. (This will keep them rounded.) **Remove** when golden brown and shiny. **Transfer** to wire rack to cool. Bagels can be double bagged and frozen to keep them longer. Makes 10 large bagels.

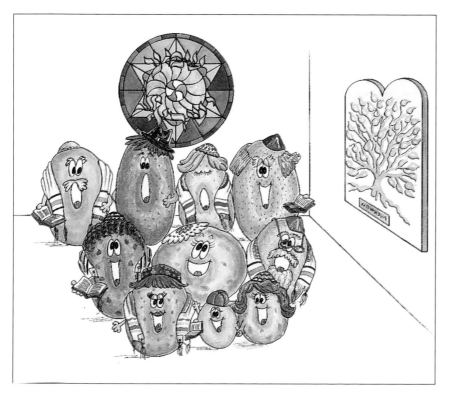

"Bagel Minyan"

When I Go to Israel I Want To . . .

Israel Is Important to the
Jewish People Because . . .

Fruits and veggies enjoy a day in the sun as they celebrate Lag Ba'omer.

Lag Ba'omer

Lag Ba'omer is a moment of joy in the fifty-day period of semi-mourning between Pesach and Shavuot. Every night for seven weeks, beginning on the second night of Pesach, we count the days until Shavuot, enjoying the freedom of our Exodus from Egypt and preparing to receive the Torah anew at Mount Sinai. Historically, the Bar Kochba Revolt, the unsuccessful Jewish rebellion against the Romans in the second century C.E., was said to have begun on Lag Ba'omer. According to tradition, there was a terrible plague during this time that killed thousands of students of the great Jewish teacher Rabbi Akiva. It is said that the plague ended on Lag Ba'omer, and so we celebrate this day when sadness turned to joy. It is customary to celebrate Lag Ba'omer outdoors, with a picnic or barbeque. Many people will also get married or cut their hair on this day. Lag Ba'omer is a wonderful opportunity to eat favorite picnic foods.

IYAR/May–June

Pareve

Grandma Ida's Potato Salad

Grandma loved potato salad almost as much as she loved to cook, and her recipe has been known to make even potato salad scoffers smile! Grandma died on Shavuot, the day after I finished writing this recipe, so it is now a part of her legacy. The secret is lots of fresh lemon juice and not too much mayonnaise! (I've added just a touch of purple onion and sweet red pepper for color.) Try this tangy, colorful salad at your next picnic! Grandma would be so happy.

INGREDIENTS	UTENSILS
2 eggs, hard-boiled	large mixing bowl
4–5 potatoes	small pot with lid
3 small or 2 large stalks celery	large pot
2 scallions	measuring spoons/cups
fresh parsley	chopping knife
1/2 sweet red bell pepper	cutting board
(optional)	vegetable peeler
1/4 purple onion	fork or slotted spoon
1–2 lemons	mixing spoon
2–3 T. mayonnaise	small strainer
spicy brown or deli mustard	
salt & pepper, to taste	

❶ **Put** eggs in a small pot, **fill** with water until eggs are just covered, **cover** pot, and **place** on stove on high heat. After water comes to a boil, **turn down** to warm and **keep** pot **covered** for 15–20 minutes. While eggs are boiling, you can start the potatoes.

❷ **Scrub** potatoes and **remove** all eyes and bad spots. DO NOT PEEL POTATOES. **Cut** potatoes in quarters and **place** in large pot of water. **Turn on** stove to high and **boil** potatoes until they are soft, not mushy. (A fork should be able to go in easily but not cause potato to completely fall apart.)

❸ **Turn off** burner for eggs. **Drain** hot water from pot carefully, using lid to keep eggs from spilling out. (Let a grown-up help you with this step!) **Refill** pot with cold tap water until eggs are covered and **set aside** to cool.

❹ While potatoes are boiling, **chop** the rest of the ingredients. **Wash** and **chop** the celery, scallions, parsley, and red pepper. **Slice** the purple onion into rings or half rings. (If you lay the onion on its side, and start slicing from one end, you will get beautiful onion rings!) **Dump** all ingredients into large mixing bowl.

❺ When potatoes are done, **turn off** burner and **remove** pot from heat. Carefully **take out** a few pieces with a fork or slotted spoon and **place** on a clean cutting board. For a healthier, more vitamin-rich salad, **leave skins on**. (To remove potato skins, **scrape** skins off with a knife or the back of a fork.) Then **cut** potatoes into bite-size chunks, **put** in mixing bowl, and **squeeze** fresh lemon juice over them, **squeezing** the lemons into a small strainer held over the bowl (to keep the lemon seeds from getting in the salad). **Repeat** this step with all the potatoes, **squeezing** lemon juice over all the pieces.

❻ **Add** 2–3 tablespoons of mayonnaise and about 1–2 teaspoons of mustard to the bowl. **Add** salt and pepper and mix well. **Slice** eggs and **mix into** salad, or **use** as garnish on top. **Adjust** seasonings to taste. Voilà! Now you're ready for a picnic!

COUNTING THE OMER

Counting the omer ties the physical freedom of Pesach and the Exodus from Egypt to the spiritual freedom of receiving the Torah on Shavuot.

Just as the Israelites counted the days and years of their journey through the desert, we count the days of our journey from Pesach to Shavuot.

IYAR/May–June

Pareve

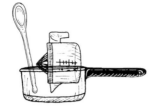

Katka's Lemonade Concentrate

My Great Aunt Katka uses lemons from her own tree in her garden in Haifa, Israel to make this delicious drink. This cooling concoction can be used with water or seltzer for a thirst-quenching summer beverage.

INGREDIENTS
1³/4 cups sugar
1 cup water
1¹/4 c. fresh-squeezed
   lemon juice

UTENSILS
hand or electric juicer
liquid measuring cup
large saucepan
mixing spoon
glass jar or container
   with lid

❶ **Combine** sugar and water in large saucepan.

❷ **Bring to** a **boil** on medium heat, **stirring constantly** until sugar is dissolved. **Turn off** heat. **Stir in** lemon juice.

❸ **Remove** from stove and **set aside** to cool.

❹ **Pour** concentrate into glass jar and **refrigerate** until ready to use. Makes about 24 ounces. Can be kept refrigerated for at least 1 week.*

❺ FOR ONE GLASS OF LEMONADE: **Pour** approximately 3–4 tablespoons of concentrate into a glass, then **add** either cold water or plain seltzer. **Adjust** amounts of water or concentrate to suit your taste.

*I've tried to freeze this as ice cubes, but the amount of sugar prevents it from freezing completely. It will, however, keep longer this way, although the cubes will remain soft. TO FREEZE, **fill** ice cube trays with concentrate, then **use** about 1¹/2 cubes per glass of water.

BOWS AND ARROWS

It is customary for children to play with toy bows and arrows on Lag Ba'omer. Why? When the Romans ruled the Land of Israel, they did not allow Jews to study Torah, and anyone caught studying would be killed. Rabbi Akiva and Rabbi Shimon bar Yochai both continued to teach their students in secret. We are told that Rabbi Akiva said, "Jews without Torah are like fish without water!" The students would disguise themselves as hunters and carry bows and arrows deep into the woods, studying Torah there with their teachers. Sometimes they hid in caves and if they were caught by the Romans, they could say they were only hunting.

FIRST HAIRCUTS

In some Jewish communities, boys who have reached the age of three get their first haircuts on Lag Ba'omer. In Israel, some people bring their children to Mt. Meron, where Rabbi Shimon bar Yochai is buried, for the ceremonial first haircut.

IYAR/May–June

Pareve

Homemade Fruity Fruit Roll

When I was growing up in northern California, we had a huge old apricot tree that grew the best tasting apricots in the whole world. We had so many of them that we dried them, used them to make jam and even made our own fruit roll. My father built a sulphur house and big wooden racks the size of doors so we could dry the apricots in the sulphur house and then in the sun. My mother would wash, pit, and cut them in half, and my father would lay them out on the racks and dry them. We dried so many that even long after the tree was gone, we still enjoyed the apricots for years. Fruit roll is fun to eat and keeps for months in the refrigerator. Take it on a hike or to your favorite picnic.

INGREDIENTS
5 c. sliced, ripe strawberries,
    peaches, apricots, or plums
1/2 c. sugar
2 T. fresh-squeezed lemon juice
    sunshine

UTENSILS
vegetable peeler
juicer
measuring cups/spoons
large saucepan
food processor or blender
2 jelly roll pans/baking
    sheets
plastic wrap/wax paper
fine mesh screen

❶ **Pit** peaches, apricots, or plums. (DO NOT PEEL plums or apricots; you may need to peel peaches.)

❷ **Cut** fruit in halves or quarters and **put** in food processor. **Process** until it makes a smooth puree.

❸ **Transfer** fruit to saucepan, **add** sugar and lemon juice, and **cook** over moderate heat, **stirring constantly, just until** mixture **boils** and sugar **dissolves. Remove** from heat and **let** mixture **cool** until tepid (lukewarm).

❹ While mixture is cooling, **cover** two large baking sheets or jelly roll pans with wide plastic wrap or wax paper. Jelly roll pans are best because they have sides. **Let** the plastic wrap or wax paper **come up** the edges, but not hang over. **Pour** puree into prepared pans, **spreading** it about 1/8 inch thick.

❺ **Cover** pans with a fine mesh screen. You can use an old window screen, but wash it well first! **Place** pans in the sun for 20 hours of sunlight or 2–3 days. **Bring** pans **in** at night. **Let cool** completely. TO STORE, **roll** leather **up** with plastic wrap or wax paper and **keep** in an airtight container in the refrigerator. It freezes well too.

What We Learned About Lag Ba'omer:

Moses on Mount Sinai.

Shavuot

Seven weeks after Pesach comes the harvest festival of Shavuot. The word Shavuot means "weeks." After leaving Egypt, the Israelites were free. But with freedom comes responsibilities. Seven weeks after leaving Egypt, the Israelites gathered at Mount Sinai and received the Torah, the book of laws that would help guide them and show them how to live and grow into a responsible people. Once the people reached the Land of Israel and settled there, they became farmers. Wheat was their most important crop. They harvested their wheat before Shavuot and would bring their first sheaves of wheat to the Temple in Jerusalem as an offering to God. These offerings were called *bikurim*, the first fruits or crops. There would be long processions, with each family or town bringing its first fruits and grain in baskets and on wagons to the Temple. Once the Temple was destroyed, Shavuot celebrations began focusing on the giving of the Torah, and new customs sprang up, like eating dairy foods and decorating homes and synagogues with flowers, leaves, and papercut decorations. In Israel today the *kibbutzim* and *moshavim* have brought back the custom of *bikurim*, with processions of tractors decorated with flowers and signs celebrating the harvest and the giving of the Torah.

SIVAN/May-June

Dairy

Bubbe's Blintzes

Bubbe, my mother's grandmother, made these blintzes on Shavuot and served them with sour cream. What makes these blintzes different from all other blintzes? They are not sweet. However, those of you with a sweet tooth can always add jam!

INGREDIENTS
PANCAKES:
1 c. cold water
1 c. flour
1 egg
1/8 t. salt
butter or margarine for frying
FILLING:
1 egg
1/2 lb. ricotta cheese
2 T. melted butter
salt (optional)

UTENSILS
electric beaters
medium mixing bowl
mixing spoon & tablespoon
measuring cups & spoons
dishcloth
spatula
small frying pan
large skillet or frying pan
pot holder
baking sheet

MAKING THE CREPES

❶ **Beat** cold water, flour, egg, and salt until batter is smooth. **Spread** a clean dishcloth on the table.

❷ **Heat** a small frying pan and **grease** lightly with butter or margarine. **Pour** in 2 tablespoons of batter and **tilt** frying pan in all directions until batter spreads evenly over the whole surface of the pan.

❸ **Fry** over low heat on **one side only**, until crepe no longer sticks to the pan—only a minute or two. (You will know it is done when it no longer looks wet or when the edges start to curl up.) **Shake** pan gently **upside down** over cloth—crepe should drop onto cloth. (If crepe sticks, either it is not quite cooked enough, or you need to add a little more butter the next time. You may need to nudge it carefully with a spatula to get it out of the pan.) **Repeat** these steps until you have used all the batter. **Place** the crepes side by side on the cloth to cool.

MAKING THE FILLING

❶ Combine egg, ricotta cheese, butter, and salt (if desired). **Spread** a little filling with a spoon on each crepe, and **fold up** sides to **form** a **square**. **Place** in pan with folds down, to stick it together.

❷ Sauté in butter, **turning** once until lightly browned on both sides. **Keep** blintzes in a single-layer on a baking sheet in a warm oven until ready to eat. **Serve** with sour cream. Makes about 14 blintzes.

Moses tries to present the Ten Commandments
to the not-so-receptive people.

SIVAN/May–June

Dairy

Grandma Gisi's Noodle Kugel

Whenever I went to my Grandma's house, she always made this favorite for me. Now you can make it too! Oh so yummy, but don't count the calories!

INGREDIENTS
8–10 oz. broad noodles
1/2 c. sugar
1/2 lb. cottage cheese*
3/4 t. vanilla
1/2 c. white raisins
3 1/2 eggs
1 c. (8 oz.) sour cream*
1/2 c. melted butter

TOPPING:
1/4 c. cornflakes, slightly crushed
1/2 t. cinnamon
1/2 t. sugar
butter

UTENSILS
large pot to boil noodles
wooden spoon
measuring cups/spoons
large mixing bowl
9 x 7-inch baking pan
   or baking dish
liquid measuring cup

*I use reduced-fat versions of these, and it still tastes delicious! Recipe can also be doubled.

❶ **Boil** noodles and **drain**.

❷ **Mix** all ingredients in large bowl.

❸ **Pour** into baking pan and **chill** in refrigerator at least 3 hours.

❹ Meanwhile **mix together** cornflakes, cinnamon, and sugar for topping. **Sprinkle** on pudding when chilled, and **dot** with a little butter.

❺ **Bake covered** at 350° (or 325° if using a glass dish) about 1 hour or until golden brown. Serves 8–10.

BOOK OF RUTH
The *Book of Ruth* is read on Shavuot. The story, like the holiday, takes place during the harvest season. Ruth, recently widowed, decides to accompany her mother-in-law Naomi to Bethlehem and eventually marries Boaz, a relative of Ruth's late husband. Ruth, who was not a Jew, chooses to follow Naomi and Naomi's God. She is often referred to as the first convert in the Bible. She became an ancestor of King David, which teaches us that anyone with dedication and commitment can become an important member of the Jewish people. When someone becomes part of the Jewish people, he or she accepts the Torah, something all Jews did at Mount Sinai and relive every Shavuot.

BLOOMING DESERT
According to legend, when the Torah was given at Mount Sinai, the entire mountain and surrounding desert bloomed with grass and flowers. Because of this legend some people decorate their homes and synagogues with flowers and leaves for Shavuot.

SIVAN/May–June

Dairy* & Pareve

Cold Strawberry Yogurt Soup

These two simple, tasty, and refreshing soups are perfect for dessert on a hot summer evening. Feel free to substitute your own favorite fruits; just follow the amounts given and go wild!

INGREDIENTS
3 c. strawberries
1/2 c. pineapple juice, cold
1 T. sugar, honey, or other sweetener
8 oz. strawberry yogurt, low fat or regular

UTENSILS
blender or food processor
paring knife
rubber scraper
can opener
measuring cups/spoons

❶ **Wash** and **remove** stems and leaves from strawberries.

❷ **Put** all ingredients in food processor or blender, and **blend** on high speed until smooth. **Serve** immediately. Makes 3 1/2 cups.

Cold Peach/Nectarine Soup

This pareve soup can be made with either peaches, nectarines, or both.

INGREDIENTS
4 peaches, peeled, pitted, & halved, or 4 nectarines, pitted & halved
1/2 c. white grape juice, cold
1 T. sugar, honey, or other sweetener
juice of 1/2 lemon
1/8 t. cinnamon

UTENSILS
blender or food processor
paring knife
vegetable peeler
rubber scraper
measuring cups/spoons

❶ **Wash**, **peel**, and **remove** pits from peaches. **Cut** into halves. If using nectarines, **leave** skins on; just **pit** them and **cut** into halves.

❷ **Measure** all ingredients into food processor or blender, and **blend** on high speed until smooth. **Serve** immediately. Makes 3 1/2 cups.

TIKKUN LEIL SHAVUOT
It is customary to stay up all night studying on erev Shavuot. Some people study a part of every book of the Torah, others read a portion of each of the other books of the Bible. There is a midrash that the Israelites were not ready to receive the Torah at Mount Sinai. By staying up all night we show that we are excited to receive the Torah.

EVERYONE WAS AT SINAI
According to tradition, the soul of every Jewish person, past, present, and future, was present at Mount Sinai, and every single person heard something unique. Only when we can combine all of those different messages will we understand revelation.

DID YOU KNOW . . .
The giving of the Ten Commandments is mentioned twice in the Torah, once in Exodus and once in Deuteronomy. Though they are almost the same, there are slight differences between the two versions.

Our Family's Favorite Shavuot Recipe/s:

My Own Ten Commandments
for How People Should Behave:

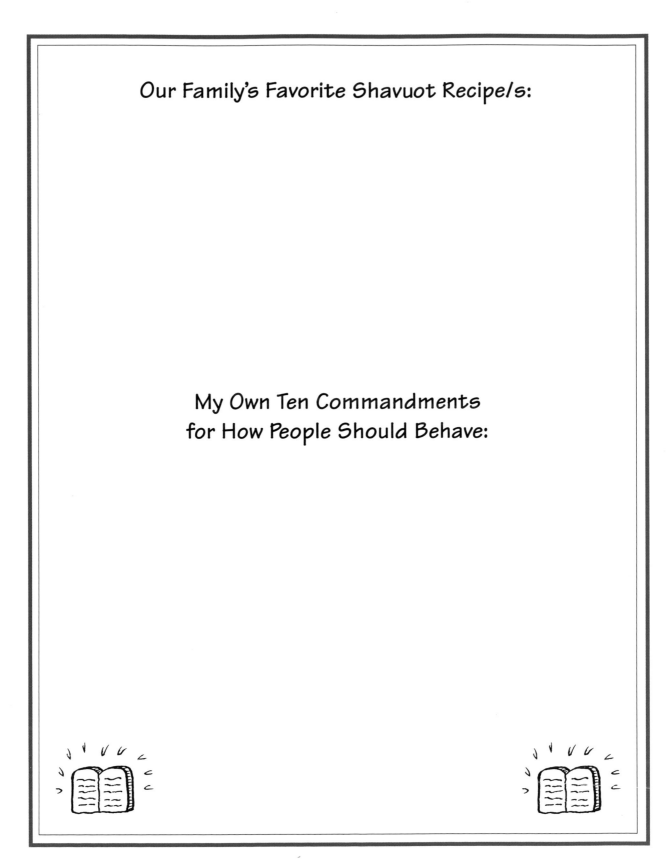

Veggies at the Western Wall.

Tishah B'av

Tishah B'Av, the ninth (*tishah*) day of the month Av, is a solemn day in the Jewish year. Tishah B'av marks the day when both the First and Second Temples in Jerusalem were destroyed and the people of Israel began their exile. The First Temple, built by King Solomon, was a grand palace where Jews from all over would come to offer sacrifices. In 586 B.C.E., it was destroyed by the Babylonian King Nebuchadnezzar and the Jews began their exile. The Second Temple was built by King Herod during the time of the Romans. This Temple was even larger and grander than the first, but it was destroyed by the Roman Emperor Titus in 70 C.E., exactly 656 years to the day after the First Temple was destroyed. The Kotel, or Western Wall, in the Old City of Jerusalem is the last remaining piece of the retaining wall of up the Second Temple. Because Tishah B'av is a day of sadness for what we have lost, many Jews refrain from doing things they enjoy, like eating, bathing, and wearing leather shoes, just like on Yom Kippur. It is a tradition to read and study books like the Book of Job and Lamentations. This day also commemorates other tragedies that the Jewish people have endured, including the second-century rebellion against the Romans, the Spanish Inquisition of 1492, and the Holocaust. Despite all the tragedies, however, the Jewish people have not only survived, but thrived. It is a mitzvah to eat a nice meal before we fast and of course have a break-the-fast afterward!

AV/July–August
Dairy

Veggie Lasagna

This recipe is chock-full of vegetables and can be made with low-fat cheeses and will still come out tasting delicious! It is a good, filling dish to bring for a potluck dinner before the fast or to break the fast. It also makes great leftovers!

INGREDIENTS
1 egg
8 oz. ricotta cheese
8 oz. cottage cheese
1/2 t. dried basil
1/2 t. dried oregano
1 box (10 oz.) chopped
    frozen spinach
3 c. (30 oz.) spaghetti
    sauce, any kind
12 pieces oven-ready
    lasagna, uncooked &
    unsoaked*
zucchini, mushrooms,
    broccoli, eggplant, etc.
12 oz. shredded mozzarella
    cheese
1/4 c. grated parmesan
    cheese
parsley flakes

UTENSILS
13 x 9 x 2-inch baking dish
medium mixing bowl
strainer
measuring cups/spoons
mixing spoon
fork
aluminum foil

*Make sure you have the kind that cooks in 40 minutes, NOT over an hour.

❶ **Preheat** the oven to 350°. In a medium bowl, **beat** one egg slightly with a fork. **Mix in** ricotta and cottage cheese. **Add** basil and oregano.

❷ **Defrost** and **cook** spinach according to package directions. **Drain** spinach well and **add** to cheese and egg mixture. **Stir** until blended.

❸ In a 13 x 9 x 2-inch baking dish, **spread** 3/4 cup spaghetti sauce. **Place** 3 pieces of uncooked pasta crosswise over sauce. **Do not overlap** pieces or let them **touch** the sides of the pan; they will expand when they are baked.

❹ **Spread** 1/3 of the ricotta mixture evenly over the pasta. **Place** a single layer of sliced zucchini, mushrooms, thinly sliced eggplant, or chopped broccoli over the cheese mixture and **sprinkle** with a little mozzarella.

❺ **Repeat** steps 3 & 4 TWO more times, **adding** whatever veggies you like best. **Top** with remaining 3 pasta pieces. **Spread** remaining sauce completely over pasta. **Sprinkle** with remaining mozzarella and parmesan cheese. **Sprinkle** top with parsley flakes.

❻ **Cover** with foil and **bake** at 350° for 30 minutes. **Remove** foil and **bake** uncovered 10–15 minutes longer or until hot and bubbly. **Let stand** 5 minutes before cutting. Makes about 10–12 servings, depending on how hungry you are!

TO PREPARE A LASAGNA AHEAD OF TIME.
❶ **Prepare** as directed above but **DO NOT BAKE. Cover** with plastic wrap, then foil. **Refrigerate** up to 48 hours **or freeze** up to 2 months.

❷ When ready to bake, **remove** plastic wrap; **replace** foil. **Bake** refrigerated lasagna at 350° for about 40 minutes and frozen lasagna about 1 hour 30 minutes, **removing** foil for the last 10 minutes of baking.

Sour Cream Apple Spice Cake

This one's a relatively easy and always tasty dessert that is a lovely addition to any holiday table. It's one of my favorites from my mother's kitchen, to yours.

INGREDIENTS
1 c. butter (2 sticks),
    softened
1^1/4 c. sugar
2 eggs
1 c. sour cream (low fat
    or regular)
1 t. vanilla
2^1/4 c. flour
1 t. baking powder
^{1}/2 t. baking soda
butter or margarine
    & flour (for pan)

TOPPING:
1 apple, peeled & diced
1 t. cinnamon
3 T. sugar
1 c. finely chopped nuts

UTENSILS
9-inch tube pan
vegetable peeler
assorted mixing bowls
rubber scraper
measuring cups & spoons
electric or hand mixer
food processor or
    chopping knife & board
sifter or strainer
wire rack

TIME FOR COMFORT
Q. What is the name of the Shabbat immediately following Tishah B'av?

A. Shabbat Nachamu, "The Shabbat of Comfort." It is called this because the Haftarah begins with the words Nachamu nachamu, "Comfort ye, My people."

After Tishah B'av and the destruction of the Temple, we need to be consoled.

❶ **Preheat** the oven to 350°. Lightly **grease** and **flour** inside of pan.

❷ **Peel**, **core**, and **finely dice** apple. **Put** apple pieces in a bowl. **Mix** cinnamon, sugar, and nuts in a separate bowl, then **add** ^{1}/2 of the nut mixture to the apple pieces and **mix**.

❸ **Cream** butter and sugar in large mixing bowl. **Add** eggs, sour cream, and vanilla and **beat well**.

❹ **Sift** dry ingredients (flour, baking powder, and baking soda) and **add** to creamed mixture. When too thick to beat, **stir** with a spoon.

❺ **Spread** half the batter in a greased and floured 9-inch tube pan. **Sprinkle** the cinnamon-apple-nut mixture on top of batter. **Add** the remaining batter to pan and **sprinkle** the remaining half of the cinnamon-apple-nut topping evenly over dough.

❻ **Bake** at 350° for about 45 minutes to 1 hour, or until a toothpick inserted in cake comes out clean. **Cool** on wire rack for about 10 minutes before removing cake from pan.

On Tishah B'av I Think About. . .

Peninah Pomegranate, Batya Banana, Brenda Broccoli, Greta Garlic, Carie Carrot, Edna Eggplant, Ora Orange, and Polly Pepper celebrate the arrival of the new moon.

Rosh Chodesh

Rosh Chodesh celebrates the appearance of the new moon. This marks the beginning of a new month in the Jewish calendar. The solar calendar we use has 365 days, the time it takes the earth to orbit the sun. But the Jewish calendar is based on a lunar cycle—how much time it takes the moon to orbit the earth—twenty-nine and a half days. Rosh Chodesh is celebrated for one or two days, depending on the length of the previous month. On Rosh Chodesh, we say special prayers in synagogue and read from the Torah. Rosh Chodesh is also a special holiday for women. In the Talmud, the moon symbolizes femininity. There is a midrash that says that when the Israelites were waiting for Moses at the foot of Mount Sinai, the people offered their jewelry and gold to Aaron so he could make the Golden Calf, and the women refused. We are told that these women were also among the first to offer help in the building of the Tabernacle. As a reward for these two acts, they were given the celebration of the new moon, during which they did no work. Today, women are reclaiming this joyous time of the month, using it for study, song, and celebration.

EVERY MONTH/On the New Moon

Dairy* or Pareve

Woman in the Moon Cookies

This recipe can also be used to make Chanukah sugar cookies, using stars and dreidels instead of moon shapes. Make sure you know where to find blue sugar crystals in your community—it can be a challenge to find anything but red and green during the holiday season! Happy Rosh Chodesh!

INGREDIENTS
1 c. sugar
1/2 t. salt
3/4 cup butter* or
   margarine, softened
1 egg
1 t. lemon juice (or
   grated lemon rind)
1 t. vanilla
3 c. flour
1 t. baking powder
colored sugar for decoration

UTENSILS
measuring cups/spoons
electric beaters
spatula
rubber scraper
assorted mixing bowls
rolling pin
large glass or cookie cutter
cookie sheets
wire cooling rack

MAKING THE DOUGH
❶ **Preheat** the oven to 350°. **Cream** sugar, salt, and butter or margarine in bowl. **Blend in** egg, lemon juice, and vanilla. **Measure** flour and baking powder. **Add** to creamed mixture. **Blend**.

FORMING THE MOON COOKIES
❷ Dough might be dry at first. Use your hands to **form** dough into a large ball. Now **roll out** dough on floured board until about 1/4 inch thick.

❸ Now **use** the open end of **a glass to cut out** round full-moon shapes. **Press down** firmly on the dough until the glass **cuts** completely through the dough. **Create** different cycles of the moon by **placing** the glass over a circle of dough and **intersecting** the circle to create new moons, half moons, crescent moons, or anything in

---

JEWISH CALENDAR
Q. Can you name all the months in the Jewish calendar... without looking through this cookbook?!

A. *Nisan, Iyar, Sivan, Tamuz, Av, Elul, Tishrei, Cheshvan, Kislev, Tevet, Shevat, Adar I, Adar II.*

BLESSING THE NEW MONTH
Beautiful blessings are recited each month on the Shabbat before Rosh Chodesh that announce the coming of the new month. We ask God to bless the new month for us and for all people with life and peace, joy and gladness, goodness and blessing. This is said while holding the Sefer Torah aloft for all to see.

between. **Use a knife to cut** circles in half to **make** half-moons.

❹ **Form** leftover dough into a ball and **roll out** again. **Repeat steps** until you have used all the dough. **Transfer** cookies carefully with a spatula to a greased cookie sheet. **Sprinkle** with colored sugar.

❺ **Bake** at 350° for 7–8 minutes. DO NOT OVERBAKE. Cookies should still be pale. **Transfer** to a wire rack **to cool**. Makes about 6 dozen cookies.

LEAP OF FAITH
Because the lunar calendar is based on twelve months of either twenty-nine or thirty days, within a few years the festival days would move back in time, and we'd be celebrating Pesach in the winter! That's why our sages added a leap month every few years (Adar II), so holidays would always fall in their proper season.

My Favorite Hebrew Month Is_____Because. . .

Blessings for Shabbat and Holidays

Shabbat Candlelighting

בָּרוּךְ אַתָּה יְיָ אֱלֹהֵינוּ מֶלֶךְ הָעוֹלָם, אֲשֶׁר קִדְּשָׁנוּ בְּמִצְוֹתָיו וְצִוָּנוּ לְהַדְלִיק נֵר שֶׁל שַׁבָּת.

Blessed are You, Adonai our God, Ruler of the universe, who makes us holy with *mitzvot* and commands us to light the Shabbat light.

Shabbat Evening *Kiddush* (Blessing over Wine)

וַיְהִי עֶרֶב וַיְהִי בֹקֶר

יוֹם הַשִּׁשִּׁי. וַיְכֻלּוּ הַשָּׁמַיִם וְהָאָרֶץ וְכָל צְבָאָם: וַיְכַל אֱלֹהִים בַּיּוֹם הַשְּׁבִיעִי מְלַאכְתּוֹ אֲשֶׁר עָשָׂה, וַיִּשְׁבֹּת בַּיּוֹם הַשְּׁבִיעִי מִכָּל מְלַאכְתּוֹ אֲשֶׁר עָשָׂה: וַיְבָרֶךְ אֱלֹהִים אֶת יוֹם הַשְּׁבִיעִי וַיְקַדֵּשׁ אֹתוֹ, כִּי בוֹ שָׁבַת מִכָּל מְלַאכְתּוֹ, אֲשֶׁר בָּרָא אֱלֹהִים לַעֲשׂוֹת:

סַבְרִי חֲבֵרַי:

בָּרוּךְ אַתָּה יְיָ אֱלֹהֵינוּ מֶלֶךְ הָעוֹלָם, בּוֹרֵא פְּרִי הַגָּפֶן.

בָּרוּךְ אַתָּה יְיָ אֱלֹהֵינוּ מֶלֶךְ הָעוֹלָם, אֲשֶׁר קִדְּשָׁנוּ בְּמִצְוֹתָיו וְרָצָה בָנוּ, וְשַׁבַּת קָדְשׁוֹ בְּאַהֲבָה וּבְרָצוֹן הִנְחִילָנוּ זִכָּרוֹן לְמַעֲשֵׂה בְרֵאשִׁית, כִּי הוּא יוֹם תְּחִלָּה לְמִקְרָאֵי קֹדֶשׁ, זֵכֶר לִיצִיאַת מִצְרָיִם, כִּי בָנוּ בָחַרְתָּ וְאוֹתָנוּ קִדַּשְׁתָּ מִכָּל הָעַמִּים, וְשַׁבַּת קָדְשְׁךָ בְּאַהֲבָה וּבְרָצוֹן הִנְחַלְתָּנוּ. בָּרוּךְ אַתָּה יְיָ, מְקַדֵּשׁ הַשַּׁבָּת.

And there was evening and there was morning—
the sixth day. The heavens and the earth, and all they contain, were completed. On the seventh day God completed the work that God had been doing. God ceased on the seventh day from all the work that God had done. Then God blessed the seventh day and called it holy, because on it God ceased from all God's work of Creation.

-Genesis 1:31-2:3

Blessed are You, Adonai our God, Ruler of the universe, who creates fruit of the vine.

Blessed are You, Adonai our God, Ruler of the universe, whose *mitzvot* add holiness to our lives, cherishing us through the gift of Your holy Shabbat granted lovingly, gladly, a reminder of Creation. It is the first among our days of sacred assembly recalling the Exodus from Egypt. Thus You have chosen us, endowing us with holiness, from among all peoples by granting us Your holy Shabbat lovingly and gladly.
Blessed are You, Adonai who hallows Shabbat.

Washing One's Hands

בָּרוּךְ אַתָּה יְיָ אֱלֹהֵינוּ מֶלֶךְ הָעוֹלָם, אֲשֶׁר קִדְּשָׁנוּ בְּמִצְוֹתָיו וְצִוָּנוּ עַל נְטִילַת יָדַיִם.

Blessed are You, Adonai our God, Ruler of the universe, who makes us holy with the *mitzvot* and commands us to wash our hands.

Hamotzi (Blessing over Bread)

בָּרוּךְ אַתָּה יְיָ אֱלֹהֵינוּ מֶלֶךְ הָעוֹלָם, הַמּוֹצִיא לֶחֶם מִן הָאָרֶץ.

Blessed are You, Adonai our God, Ruler of the universe, who brings forth bread from the earth.

Blessings for Children

For sons:

יְשִׂימְךָ אֱלֹהִים כְּאֶפְרַיִם וְכִמְנַשֶּׁה.

May God give you the blessings of Ephraim and Menasheh.

For daughters:

יְשִׂימֵךְ אֱלֹהִים כְּשָׂרָה, רִבְקָה, רָחֵל, וְלֵאָה.

May God give you the blessings of Sarah, Rebecca, Rachel, and Leah.

Continue for all:

יְבָרֶכְךָ יְיָ וְיִשְׁמְרֶךָ. יָאֵר יְיָ פָּנָיו אֵלֶיךָ וִיחֻנֶּךָּ. יִשָּׂא יְיָ פָּנָיו אֵלֶיךָ וְיָשֵׂם לְךָ שָׁלוֹם.

May God bless you and keep you. May God show you favor and be gracious to you. May God show you kindness and grant you peace.

Shehecheyanu (Before Doing Something for the First Time)

בָּרוּךְ אַתָּה יְיָ אֱלֹהֵינוּ מֶלֶךְ הָעוֹלָם, שֶׁהֶחֱיָנוּ וְקִיְּמָנוּ וְהִגִּיעָנוּ לַזְּמַן הַזֶּה.

Blessed are You, Adonai our God, who has kept us alive and sustained us and enabled us to reach this season.

Kiddush for Shabbat Lunch

וְשָׁמְרוּ בְנֵי יִשְׂרָאֵל אֶת הַשַּׁבָּת, לַעֲשׂוֹת אֶת הַשַּׁבָּת לְדֹרֹתָם בְּרִית עוֹלָם. בֵּינִי וּבֵין בְּנֵי יִשְׂרָאֵל אוֹת הִיא לְעֹלָם, כִּי שֵׁשֶׁת יָמִים עָשָׂה יְיָ אֶת הַשָּׁמַיִם וְאֶת הָאָרֶץ, וּבַיּוֹם הַשְּׁבִיעִי שָׁבַת וַיִּנָּפַשׁ.

עַל כֵּן בֵּרַךְ יְיָ אֶת יוֹם הַשַּׁבָּת וַיְקַדְּשֵׁהוּ.

סַבְרִי חֲבֵרִי:
בָּרוּךְ אַתָּה יְיָ אֱלֹהֵינוּ מֶלֶךְ הָעוֹלָם, בּוֹרֵא פְּרִי הַגָּפֶן.

The people Israel shall observe Shabbat, to maintain it as an everlasting covenant through all generations. It is a sign between Me and the people Israel for all time, that in six days Adonai made the heavens and the earth, and on the seventh day God ceased from work and rested.

-Exodus 31:16-17

Therefore Adonai blessed the day of Shabbat and made it holy.

-Exodus 20:11

Blessed are You, Adonai our God, Ruler of the universe, who creates fruit of the vine.

Candlelighting for Festivals and Yom Kippur

בָּרוּךְ אַתָּה יְיָ אֱלֹהֵינוּ מֶלֶךְ הָעוֹלָם, אֲשֶׁר קִדְּשָׁנוּ בְּמִצְוֹתָיו וְצִוָּנוּ לְהַדְלִיק נֵר שֶׁל

For Festivals: יוֹם טוֹב.

For Yom Kippur: יוֹם הַכִּפּוּרִים.

Blessed are You, Adonai our God, Ruler of the universe, who makes us holy with the *mitzvot* and commands us to light the Festival light (Yom Kippur light).

Evening *Kiddush* for Festivals (Pesach, Shavuot, Sukot)

(Add text in parentheses on Shabbat)

(וַיְהִי עֶרֶב וַיְהִי בֹקֶר יוֹם הַשִּׁשִּׁי:
וַיְכֻלּוּ הַשָּׁמַיִם וְהָאָרֶץ וְכָל צְבָאָם: וַיְכַל אֱלֹהִים בַּיּוֹם הַשְּׁבִיעִי מְלַאכְתּוֹ אֲשֶׁר עָשָׂה, וַיִּשְׁבֹּת בַּיּוֹם הַשְּׁבִיעִי מִכָּל מְלַאכְתּוֹ אֲשֶׁר עָשָׂה: וַיְבָרֶךְ אֱלֹהִים אֶת יוֹם הַשְּׁבִיעִי וַיְקַדֵּשׁ אֹתוֹ, כִּי בוֹ שָׁבַת מִכָּל מְלַאכְתּוֹ, אֲשֶׁר בָּרָא אֱלֹהִים לַעֲשׂוֹת:)

סַבְרִי חַבְרַי:

סַבְרִי חַבְרַי:
בָּרוּךְ אַתָּה יְיָ אֱלֹהֵינוּ מֶלֶךְ הָעוֹלָם, בּוֹרֵא פְּרִי הַגָּפֶן.
בָּרוּךְ אַתָּה יְיָ אֱלֹהֵינוּ מֶלֶךְ הָעוֹלָם, אֲשֶׁר בָּחַר בָּנוּ וְרוֹמְמָנוּ מִכָּל לָשׁוֹן,
וְקִדְּשָׁנוּ בְּמִצְוֹתָיו. וַתִּתֶּן לָנוּ יְיָ אֱלֹהֵינוּ בְּאַהֲבָה (שַׁבָּתוֹת לִמְנוּחָה וּ) מוֹעֲדִים
לְשִׂמְחָה, חַגִּים וּזְמַנִּים לְשָׂשׂוֹן, אֶת יוֹם (הַשַּׁבָּת הַזֶּה וְאֶת יוֹם)

On Pesach:	חַג הַמַּצּוֹת הַזֶּה. זְמַן חֵרוּתֵנוּ
On Shavuot:	חַג הַשָּׁבֻעוֹת הַזֶּה. זְמַן מַתַּן תּוֹרָתֵנוּ
On Sukot:	חַג הַסֻּכּוֹת הַזֶּה. זְמַן שִׂמְחָתֵנוּ
On Simchat Torah:	הַשְּׁמִינִי חַג הָעֲצֶרֶת הַזֶּה. זְמַן שִׂמְחָתֵנוּ

(בְּאַהֲבָה) מִקְרָא קֹדֶשׁ, זֵכֶר לִיצִיאַת מִצְרָיִם: כִּי בָנוּ בָחַרְתָּ, וְאוֹתָנוּ קִדַּשְׁתָּ מִכָּל
הָעַמִּים (וְשַׁבָּת) וּמוֹעֲדֵי קָדְשֶׁךָ (בְּאַהֲבָה וּבְרָצוֹן) בְּשִׂמְחָה וּבְשָׂשׂוֹן הִנְחַלְתָּנוּ: בָּרוּךְ
אַתָּה יְיָ מְקַדֵּשׁ (הַשַּׁבָּת וְ) יִשְׂרָאֵל וְהַזְּמַנִּים:

(Add text in parentheses on Shabbat)

(And there was evening and there was morning—
the sixth day. The heavens and the earth, and all they contain, were completed. On the
seventh day God completed the work that God had been doing. God ceased on the
seventh day from all the work that God had done. Then God blessed the seventh day
and called it holy, because on it God ceased from all God's work of Creation.)
-Genesis 1:31-2:3

Blessed are You, Adonai our God, Ruler of the universe, who creates
fruit of the vine.

Blessed are You, Adonai our God, Ruler of the universe, who has chosen
and distinguished us from among all others by adding holiness to our
lives with Your mitzvot. Lovingly have You given us the gift of (Shabbat
for rest and) Festivals for joy and holidays for happiness, among them
(this Shabbat and) this day of

On Pesach: Pesach, the festival of our liberation,
On Shavuot: Shavuot, the festival of Your giving us the Torah,
On Sukot: Sukot, the festival of our joy,
On Simchat Torah: Simchat Torah, the festival of our joy,

a day of sacred assembly recalling the Exodus from Egypt. Thus You
have chosen us, endowing us with holiness, from among all peoples by
granting us Your holy (Shabbat and) Your hallowed Festivals (lovingly
and gladly) in happiness and joy. Blessed are You, Adonai who hallows
(Shabbat and) the people Israel and the Festivals.

When Dipping Apples or Challah in Honey:

יְהִי רָצוֹן מִלְּפָנֶיךָ יְיָ אֱלֹהֵינוּ וֵאלֹהֵי אֲבוֹתֵינוּ וְאִמּוֹתֵינוּ שֶׁתְּחַדֵּשׁ עָלֵינוּ שָׁנָה טוֹבָה וּמְתוּקָה.

May it be Your will, Adonai our God and God of our ancestors, that we be blessed with a good and sweet new year.

Chanukah Candlelighting

בָּרוּךְ אַתָּה יְיָ אֱלֹהֵינוּ מֶלֶךְ הָעוֹלָם, אֲשֶׁר קִדְּשָׁנוּ בְּמִצְוֹתָיו וְצִוָּנוּ לְהַדְלִיק נֵר שֶׁל חֲנֻכָּה.

בָּרוּךְ אַתָּה יְיָ אֱלֹהֵינוּ מֶלֶךְ הָעוֹלָם, שֶׁעָשָׂה נִסִּים לַאֲבוֹתֵינוּ וּלְאִמּוֹתֵינוּ בַּיָּמִים הָהֵם בַּזְּמַן הַזֶּה.

On the first night:

בָּרוּךְ אַתָּה יְיָ אֱלֹהֵינוּ מֶלֶךְ הָעוֹלָם, שֶׁהֶחֱיָנוּ וְקִיְּמָנוּ וְהִגִּיעָנוּ לַזְּמַן הַזֶּה.

Blessed are You, Adonai our God, Ruler of the universe, who makes us holy with the *mitzvot* and commanded us to light the Chanukah lights.

Blessed are You, Adonai our God, Ruler of the universe, who performed miracles for our ancestors in those days at this time.

On the first night: Blessed are You, Adonai our God, who has kept us alive and sustained us and enabled us to reach this season.

Sitting in a *Sukah*

בָּרוּךְ אַתָּה יְיָ אֱלֹהֵינוּ מֶלֶךְ הָעוֹלָם, אֲשֶׁר קִדְּשָׁנוּ בְּמִצְוֹתָיו וְצִוָּנוּ לֵישֵׁב בַּסֻּכָּה.

Blessed are You, Adonai our God, Ruler of the universe, who makes us holy with the *mitzvot* and commanded us to dwell in the *sukah*.

Shaking the *Lulav*

בָּרוּךְ אַתָּה יְיָ אֱלֹהֵינוּ מֶלֶךְ הָעוֹלָם, אֲשֶׁר קִדְּשָׁנוּ בְּמִצְוֹתָיו, וְצִוָּנוּ עַל נְטִילַת לוּלָב.

When shaking it for the first time of the year:

בָּרוּךְ אַתָּה יְיָ אֱלֹהֵינוּ מֶלֶךְ הָעוֹלָם, שֶׁהֶחֱיָנוּ וְקִיְּמָנוּ וְהִגִּיעָנוּ לַזְּמַן הַזֶּה.

Blessed are You, Adonai our God, Ruler of the universe, who makes us holy with the *mitzvot* and commanded us to wave the *lulav*.

When shaking it for the first time of the year: Blessed are You, Adonai our God, who has kept us alive and sustained us and enabled us to reach this season.

Before Eating Food (Other Than Bread) Prepared from Grains

בָּרוּךְ אַתָּה יְיָ אֱלֹהֵינוּ מֶלֶךְ הָעוֹלָם, בּוֹרֵא מִינֵי מְזוֹנוֹת.

Blessed are You, Adonai our God, Ruler of the universe, Creator of various kinds of nourishment.

Before Eating Other Foods and Drink

בָּרוּךְ אַתָּה יְיָ אֱלֹהֵינוּ מֶלֶךְ הָעוֹלָם, שֶׁהַכֹּל נִהְיֶה בִּדְבָרוֹ.

Blessed are You, Adonai our God, Ruler of the universe, by whose word all things come into being.

Before Eating Food That Grows in the Ground

בָּרוּךְ אַתָּה יְיָ אֱלֹהֵינוּ מֶלֶךְ הָעוֹלָם, בּוֹרֵא פְּרִי הָאֲדָמָה.

Blessed are You, Adonai our God, Ruler of the universe, Creator of the fruit of the ground.

Before Eating Fruit from a Tree

בָּרוּךְ אַתָּה יְיָ אֱלֹהֵינוּ מֶלֶךְ הָעוֹלָם, בּוֹרֵא פְּרִי הָעֵץ.

Blessed are You, Adonai our God, Ruler of the universe, Creator of the fruit of the tree.

Upon Smelling Fragrant Fruit

בָּרוּךְ אַתָּה יְיָ אֱלֹהֵינוּ מֶלֶךְ הָעוֹלָם, הַנּוֹתֵן רֵיחַ טוֹב בַּפֵּרוֹת.

Blessed are You, Adonai our God, Ruler of the universe, who gives a pleasant fragrance to fruits.